OUR FOREST LEGACY:

A History of Antrim County Municipal Forest Management

MISSION POINT PRESS

Published by Mission Point Press
2554 Chandler Rd.
Traverse City, MI 49696
(231) 421-9513
www.MissionPointPress.com

Book design: Sarah Meiers

ISBN: 978-1-961302-52-5
Library of Congress Control Number: 2024904058

Printed in the United States of America

OUR FOREST LEGACY:

A History of Antrim County Municipal Forest Management

MIKE MERIWETHER

MISSION POINT PRESS

CONTENTS

FOREWORD

IT IS MY PLEASURE TO WRITE THE FOREWORD for the first book that tells the story of our Antrim County forests. Three topics come to mind about this book: my experience working with the author over the years, the importance of the history in this publication, and the precious value of our forests.

Working with the Antrim Conservation District's county forester, Mike Meriwether, is never dull. We've planted ten thousand oak trees in a matter of days, inspected beaver dams, plotted new trails, created research experiments, sold countless trees at our sales, and so much more. We've taught thousands of adults and kids about trees in person and with our multimedia platforms, and through it all I have continually admired his dedication and commitment to his work.

Mike has the kind of demeanor any boss would love; he's easy to speak to and listen to, is a terrific teacher, and is a man full of knowledge that few will ever get to appreciate in the ways that I and the staff have through our work at the ACD. He is an important asset who has increased our land holdings with care and continually promotes our ongoing conservation goals. There are few in Antrim County, and likely in Michigan, who have the heart for nature and the wisdom of the woods that Mike Meriwether has.

While this book reveals the legacy that created our forests, you will also find strategy, wisdom, and wonderful historical knowledge that you won't find anywhere else. You will see extremely smart decisions from past county commissioners who had the vision and foresight to protect natural areas for the public and to promote economic growth. The value of trees to the environment and our future is priceless.

Forests are more than a thing to cut down to create a pretty view. Forests are important habitats. Forests matter to our health and welfare. Forests have economic power. These things are finely balanced and measured by the good forester and steward of the land. Mike Meriwether, Walter Kilpatrick, and Warren Studley are just a few of the names that will go down in the natural resource history of Antrim County. Their work demonstrates how the forests are managed in a good way and how their conservation efforts have paid off in many more ways than the dollar.

Antrim County residents and visitors can enjoy amazing public properties due to good decisions, and because of this book it is my hope that they will appreciate the value and importance of land and forest management even more. May we all respect the value of our public property and remember the legacy of the many people who made caring for our natural resources in Antrim County a priority.

The health of our woods, water, and wildlife must be a high area of concern for leadership from the local to national level. The Antrim Conservation District strives to conserve, protect, educate, and inform the public about our natural resources. I trust that this book will go a long way in helping our service mission by helping readers learn about the land and the people who helped make Antrim County an amazing place to live in and visit. My deepest thanks go to all who care and act to preserve our forest legacy.

—Melissa Zelenak
Antrim Conservation District, Executive Director

PREFACE

EIGHTY-SEVEN YEARS AGO, ANTRIM COUNTY began acquiring municipal forest property. Over this period, these properties have provided countless recreational and environmental benefits, becoming the building blocks for some of the county's most valuable assets.

This book began as a short report that summarized the years of forestry activities within Antrim County. The primary focus was on forest lands owned by the county. However, there is much to be said regarding acquired natural areas, parks, and private ownership as well. Those that reviewed the report suggested that it be expanded and put into a book format.

I was given the opportunity and responsibility of oversight for the county forests by the County Commissioners in 1994. Before that, there were many people involved with the stewardship of these properties. I will likely not be able to acknowledge all of them. What a special gift they have left for us all!

It is not my intention to account for the historical uses and abuses of our Michigan forests; there is much documentation on this subject. One such resource is a book written by Dave Dempsey called *Ruin and Recovery*, which tells the great story of Michigan's cycles of resource exploitation and conservation efforts from the early days of statehood in 1837 to the relative present day.

The forest land acreages currently owned by the county, like all of Michigan's forests, were at one time high-graded, cutover, burned, farmed, and generally abused throughout the late 1800s and early 1900s.

To say that the county received land that was in disrepair is an understatement. Erosion due to poor road placements, wetland destruction, conversion to agriculture and subsequent abandonment, low stocking levels, and poor-quality trees were common within many of our forests.

The forests in Antrim County are second-growth forests. They originated from naturally producing forests after being cut over or in some cases were re-planted with trees. The county has spent eighty-seven years improving its forested properties.

Some of these historical abuses are still influencing forest management. Today our forests are impacted by devastating invasive species such as emerald ash borer and beech bark disease; other pests are on the horizon as well. These will likely have equal—or perhaps even greater—influence on our future forest management.

Antrim County does not have a vast land holding. It does have enough to demonstrate what can be accomplished through wise use and good management.

INTRODUCTION

ANTRIM COUNTY HAS A LONG HISTORY OF LAND ACQUISITIONS and conservation. The county owns more than five thousand acres of public land devoted to various public usage. Roughly 90% of these properties have been devoted to forestry and the protection of natural areas and park lands. Antrim County is the second largest owner of community forest lands in the State of Michigan after Gogebic County.

> Today over eighty years of sustainable forest management can be viewed on the properties owned by Antrim County.

The Antrim County Board of Commissioners and many others had a vision for the future. Initially they wanted to provide forestry educational tools for private landowners, groups, and schools seeking to implement sustainable forestry practices on their own properties (remember conservation was in its infancy in the 1930s and '40s). The purchase of community forests allowed them to implement conservation practices that could be replicated on other privately owned lands. These practices included tree planting, forest stand improvements, erosion control, and wildlife habitat improvements. Today over eighty years of sustainable forest management can be viewed on the properties owned by Antrim County.

In addition, the county wanted to protect the scenic beauty of the county, provide public recreation opportunities for future generations, and provide sustainable forests. These community forest acquisitions began the foundation on which our county forests and future acquisitions were built. Perhaps most importantly, these land acquisitions also fostered a land-stewardship ethic within the community that has continued to this day.

Since 1939, the county has purchased or acquired more than forty individual parcels of community forest properties as well as nine other properties dedicated to parks and recreation, education, and natural area protection. By partnering with private individuals, nonprofit organizations, townships, and state and federal agencies, they have invested millions of dollars in public properties aimed at conservation, education, recreation, and natural resource protection.

Properties owned by Antrim County represent only 1.36% of the total acres in the county, but their impact on our county and communities are immeasurable.

Conserved Land	Acres	General Description
Community Forest Lands	3,056.8	Lands received from State of Michigan under the Municipal Forestry Act.
Natural Areas	1,667.00	Land dedicated to resource protection, education, and recreational activities.
Park Lands	82.7	Properties dedicated as campgrounds, day parks, and recreational use.
Industrial Lands	537.86	Land dedicated to industrial or community usage. Antrim County Airport and Meadow Brook Medical Care Facility.
TOTAL	5,344.36	

Table 1: Antrim County Ownerships

All the properties described within Table 1 contain forested acreage. Community forest lands, also called municipal forest or school forest, are where most of the intensive forest management activities occur. Natural areas and park land acreages receive periodic treatment with unique forest management prescriptions. Even industrial properties have received some forest management.

Through its cooperative agreements with the Antrim Conservation District, the county has also been able to provide private land assistance, county forest land management, and deliver many environmental projects within the community.

UNDERSTANDING COUNTY-OWNED LANDS

The county has a complex network of properties with unique attributes. The Antrim County Board of Commissioners is responsible for overseeing county-owned properties. County properties can be generally categorized into community forests, natural areas, parks, and industrial lands.

Conserved community forest lands, natural lands, and park lands provide a multitude of benefits to its citizens. These benefits include habitat for flora and fauna, recreational and sightseeing opportunities, filtration for air and water quality, protection of open space, and the production of forest products. These lands serve as an educational tool for private landowners, groups, and schools seeking to implement sustainable forestry practices on their own properties.

There are many overlapping uses which include recreation, forestry, and the protection of natural resources. There are also shared jurisdictional responsibilities. For example: the Glacial Hills Natural Area—one of the larger county forests. It is an actively managed forest where trees are periodically harvested. In addition, intensive recreational activities have been allowed on the property. It has been cooperatively agreed that the Friends of Glacial Hills will be responsible for the trail maintenance and the Antrim Conservation District Forester will be responsible for the natural resource management.

Our Community Forests

In 1931, the Michigan Legislature passed the Municipal Forest Act (Community Forest Act) authorizing the Department of Conservation the ability to convey tax-reverted lands to schools and other units of government.

OUR NATURAL AREA FORESTS

Our natural area properties are properties purchased, donated, or designated by the county board of commissioners (BOC) as natural areas. The BOC has written agreements with various nonprofit organizations to manage the county's natural areas: Grass River Natural Area, Inc., Friends of Glacial Hills Pathway, and Friends of Antrim Creek Natural Area. They function as resource protection, provide educational opportunities and recreational sites.

PARK LANDS

Antrim County has several properties which have been purchased or acquired for the purposes of providing day park usage, camping and other recreational activities. In 2021, the county hired a parks director to oversee and administer activities occurring on our park lands.

INDUSTRIAL LANDS

These are properties owned by the county for specific public usage. The Antrim County Airport is managed by the airport manager, and Meadow Brook Medical Care Facility is managed by the Meadow Brook Governing Board/Antrim County Health & Human Services Board. The county also maintains its administrative and courthouse properties through its maintenance department.

Antrim County Commissioners

The Antrim County Commissioners have a long-standing commitment to managing natural resources. Their long-term vision for all county-owned forest lands is maintaining sustainable and beautiful forests that are vigorous, stable, and diverse.

Antrim Conservation District

The Antrim Conservation District (ACD), through a cooperative agreement with Antrim County, is responsible for the management and maintenance of county forest lands. The ACD forester maintains these properties through its forestry program.

Conservation Districts—General Information

Michigan Conservation Districts (CDs) are local providers of natural resource management services. Created by the USDA in response to the 1930s dust bowl, conservation districts are local units of government that utilize state, federal, local, and private sector resources to solve today's conservation challenges. Because best conservation practices vary widely depending on the region they're practiced in, conservation districts were formed so that decisions on conservation issues could be made at the local level by local people, with additional technical assistance provided by governmental-affiliated organizations. Each of Michigan's eighty-three counties is represented by at least one conservation district. For more on Michigan's conservation districts go to MACD.org.

ACQUISITION AND CONSERVATION HISTORY

In 1929, the Michigan State Cooperative Extension Service held a conference aimed at encouraging, promoting, and fostering an educational program by the establishment of school and community forests.

In 1931, the Michigan Legislature passed the Municipal Forest Act (*Community Forest Act*) authorizing the Department of Conservation (DNR) the ability to convey tax-reverted land to schools and other units of government.

> Perhaps most importantly, these land acquisitions also fostered a land stewardship ethic within the community that has continued to this day.

Antrim County acquired its first forest property in 1935. The property is 160 acres, located east of Mancelona, and was referred to as the "Hawk Lake Forest"—it's still currently referred to as such. In 1935, Arvid Johnson, a member of the Antrim County Board of Supervisors, helped secure the property. Mr. Johnson also initiated the planting of pine on the parcel.

In 1938, MSU hired Walter Kirkpatrick as the Agricultural Extension Agent. Mr. Kirkpatrick initiated the acquisition of most of Antrim County's forest lands. Mr. Kirkpatrick convinced the county supervisors to pursue tax-reverted lands and place them in public ownership with the county. Mr. Kirkpatrick also facilitated the purchase of several school forest properties. Central Lake, Ellsworth, and Mancelona schools all own properties today through the efforts of Mr. Kirkpatrick.

Walter Kirkpatrick worked as Antrim County's Extension Agent from 1938–1968. His accomplishments and vision should be recognized. These acquisitions began the foundation on which our county forests and future acquisitions were built. Perhaps most importantly, these land acquisitions also fostered a land stewardship ethic within the community that has continued to this day.

Before his passing, Mr. Kirkpatrick was able to pen a summary of his time working to acquire and manage our county forest lands. Historical files have been archived at the MSU library.

With a stewardship ethic in place and a growing appreciation within the community to protect special places within the county, other projects and acquisitions were accomplished.

Acquisition of properties by the county has been controversial at times. Some see only dollar values relative to lost tax revenues. Others believe there is already enough public land acreage within the county. Why would

STATE OF MICHIGAN

DEPARTMENT OF CONSERVATION
LANSING 13
GERALD E. EDDY, DIRECTOR

October 15, 1952

Case No. 26960-S

Mr. Walter G. Kirkpatrick
County Agricultural Agent
Bellaire, Michigan

Dear Sir:

The Commission has approved your county's application for parts of Government Lot 7, Section 1, T 30 N, R 8 W. Will you kindly send in the nominal consideration of $1.00 and deed will be forwarded.

Very truly yours,

H. S. GIBBS
Lands Division

HSG:emd

the county need to own property? Despite some opposition, the county continued to expand its land holdings throughout from the 1950s into the 2000s.

The cost to acquire tax-reverted lands from the MDNR was $1 per deed. Other acquired parcels took advantage of state grant funds, such as the Michigan Trust Fund, a fund set up using oil and gas revenues to acquire public properties for recreational purposes and resource protection projects. Matching funds were often required to access grant dollars. On occasion, the county acquired the property through purchase or private gift. The twenty-acre Prince property, and several parcels within the Grass River Natural Area, are examples of gifted property.

The 1930s-1940s

Michigan State University, through its extension agents, began utilizing county forest lands to demonstrate forest practices that could be used on private lands.

The 160 acres in Mancelona Township, known as Hawk Lake Forest, was the first acquisition in 1935. There is some documentation that Christmas trees were originally established here. Some attempts to demonstrate the shearing and marketing of Christmas trees occurred around 1936–1940. It is unclear where and how many trees were planted for Christmas tree production. In 1936, 3,000 jack pines

Herb, Florence, and Richard Reiley planting trees

and 108,000 red pines were established on this parcel. The property was used as a demonstration site for tree planting and private landowner tours.

The 1940s were a remarkable time for acquisition. Thirty individual parcels were acquired. As parcels were acquired, stewardship activities followed. At this time a few tree plantings were established.

The first recorded sale of wood products occurred in 1943. This thinning occurred on the properties in Banks Township, now known as the Barnes Park property. William McLachlin and Richard Gribi agreed to cut, remove, and pay for pulpwood and stovewood removal from the property. The payment was $1.00 per cord and $0.34 for stovewood. "Cut all pulpwood and stovewood from such property as may be practical and considered to be of a good forestry practice."

Barnes Park

Barnes Park (1938) is a notable acquisition described by Walter Kirkpatrick. Mr. Kirkpatrick described the purchase of the sixty-five-acre parcel as follows: "The Antrim County Park (or Barnes Park) had been offered to the County, for the 'huge' price of $1,000. After much-heated discussion, the board voted to purchase the property. The vote was 8 to 7."

It was fascinating that the $1,000 asking price represented 6% of the county's operating fund for that year. The purchase was highly controversial at the time, to say the least. After the purchase of the park property, the county was able to obtain the surrounding acreages through the municipal forest program. In 1940, spruce and pine trees were planted within the park and on the municipal properties. In 2010, a forest interpretive trail was constructed providing recreational access to the surrounding forest lands.

Today, the park and the surrounding forest lands are irreplaceable assets for the county and its visitors.

The 1950s

The county acquired eleven additional community forest parcels in the 1950s. These included parcels in Mancelona, Forest Home, Echo, and Star Townships. Perhaps most notable was the additional 45.70 acres added to the parcel now known as Mohrmann Park.

In 1952, the county began planting trees on several parcels. Pine seedlings (4,248) were established on the Del Mason Road parcel. Trees (13,300) were established on the Skinkle Road parcel and trees (8,900) were planted on the Valley Road property east of Mancelona. The cost of establishing these plantations was $235. All these plantations exist today. They have been thinned several times since their establishment.

Several timber stand improvement projects were conducted throughout the 1950s. The first project described by Mr. Kirkpatrick was conducted on the forty-acre Hemstreet property west of the Bellaire School. The cut was set up as a demonstration area. Trees were marked by the MSU forester, and workers from the Antrim County Farm (forerunner to Meadow Brook) cut the trees and utilized them to heat the county facility for the next few years.

In addition to timber stand improvement projects, several properties had logs removed. At this time, logs were removed on a diameter-limit basis—here all trees above sixteen inches were harvested for logs. Today, the industry still prefers to harvest trees on a diameter-limit basis.

The county has moved away from diameter-limit cutting. Today, a more selective management approach is taken within most of the northern hardwood forest lands under county supervision.

The 1960s

Most of our forest lands received treatment in the 1960s. Timber stand improvement projects were conducted on most of the county-owned properties. The county took advantage of federal dollars available through the Agricultural Stabilization Conservation Service (ASCS) to pay for thinning projects.

County forests were growing and recovering. Trees planted in the late '30s and '40s were now beginning to reach sizes and densities that would require thinning. Cutover properties were beginning to recover and stand densities were increasing.

At this time, monies from governmental grants were used to hire cutters. They would cut and stack mostly pulpwood products, then the products were sold to pulp mills. The American Packaging Corporation was the primary buyer of the pulpwood products produced in Antrim County at the time. These products were

Warren Studley and unknown

loaded on train cars owned by the Chesapeake and Ohio Railway and shipped by rail to the American Packaging Corporation in Filer City, Michigan.

One of the first commercial log sales occurred in 1962 on the Kearney Section 6 property, with bids being solicited for the purchase of standing timber. The cutting parameters were as follows: "Maple, basswood, and hemlock can be cut over 16 inches in diameter at breast height (DBH). Beech and elm can be cut 10 inches and over and all other tree species 10 inches and over." Cull trees were marked and were to be girdled.

A second timber sale was conducted on the Forest Home Township property. Jack Lockwood, the Michigan Department of Conservation forester, marked 260 trees for harvest.

The cutting of stovewood was allowed on many of the forested properties. Stovewood was sold for $0.25 per face cord. Primarily dead trees were cut—some live trees for thinning were marked.

The county utilized federal dollars through the USDA Agricultural Stabilization Conservation Service (ASCS) to implement conservation practices such as crop tree release in the planted pine plantations, girdling cull trees, planting trees, and

timber stands improvement cutting. The county enrolled hundreds of acres of its forest lands. Herb Reiley organized cutting crews and implemented many of the improvement cutting projects for the county.

In 1968, twenty-thousand red pines were added to previous plantings on the forty acres off Valley Road in Mancelona Township.

The 1960s ushered in a conservation era within the nation. Agricultural and forestry education in Antrim County was no different.

In 1966, Warren Studley, while employed by the USDA Soil Conservation Service (SCS), completed the first inventory of county forest lands. The inventory included soils, tree species, and some notes on stocking levels and general treatment recommendations.

Commercial farming was still relatively new to Antrim County, and Warren Studley was the driving force behind the implementation of improved agricultural practices within the county. The federal government provided funds and technical expertise to farmers who were interested in implementing new concepts on their farms. An example would be the use of cover crops, rotational grazing, manure waste usage, soil testing, windbreaks, and the like.

Among Mr. Studley's many accomplishments were the creation of the Grass River Natural Area, the Antrim County Prime Forest Land Mapping Project, and a USDA grant (PL 566 grant) for $2.5 million federal, which was targeted at water quality, forestry, and agricultural practices within the Elk River Chain of Lakes Watershed. Warren Studley left a lasting impact on Antrim County.

The 1970s

The most significant event in the 1970s was the $100,000 federal grant received from the U.S. Department of Labor in 1975–76. MSU Extension Agent Burt Stanley and Soil Conservation Service Agent Warren Studley investigated the possibility of using Comprehensive Education Training Act (CETA) funds to hire a forester to create a work plan. The county hired Lee Ekstrom, a forest consultant, to write forest management plans for county owned parcels.

At the same time, Antrim County Planner Gary Rogers prepared some proposals to be submitted on behalf of the planning commission for possible federal funding regarding make-work or labor-intensive projects for underemployed individuals.

Possibly most important—in the short run—was the need to provide short-term jobs to unemployed Antrim County residents. In March of 1976, the unemployment rate was 15.6% in Antrim County.

Stanley, Studley, Rogers, and Ekstrom put the details together and Antrim County was awarded the EDA grant in 1976. The plan called for the county to hire twenty-one people to implement timber stand improvement cutting on 1,900 acres of county-owned forest lands. In addition, fifty thousand trees were planted and some crop tree pruning projects were completed on some of the existing pine plantations.

Forest management plans were prepared by Mr. Ekstrom for each parcel of forest land owned by the county. Mr. Ekstrom identified stocking levels, species percentages, soil types, and other significant features of each forest. Recommendations were also made for each forest property.

The stand-improvement cutting had several benefits. First, our forests received much-needed thinning and improvements. Second, cull trees were dropped and left behind in the forest. This provided much-needed fuel and stove woodcutting opportunities for the community. Third, employment opportunities were provided to the community in a time of need.

The county extension office continued to be the driving force regarding forest management on county forest lands in the 1970s. The extension agent, Karl Larson, and Burt Stanley utilized area forester Jack Lockwood for timber sale assistance on behalf of the county. The cutting of firewood and stovewood was a frequent activity on county lands. The extension agents issued and monitored firewood cutting permits for the county.

In 1976, the county issued fifty-eight firewood cutting permits on county forest lands. The firewood became available through the timber stand improvement cutting project.

Grass River Natural Area

Another notable acquisition is the Grass River Natural Area. In 1969, with tremendous contributions from individuals, businesses, foundations, and governmental agencies, the acquisition of several parcels would eventually make up the Grass River Natural Area. Like Barnes Park, this was significant at the time.

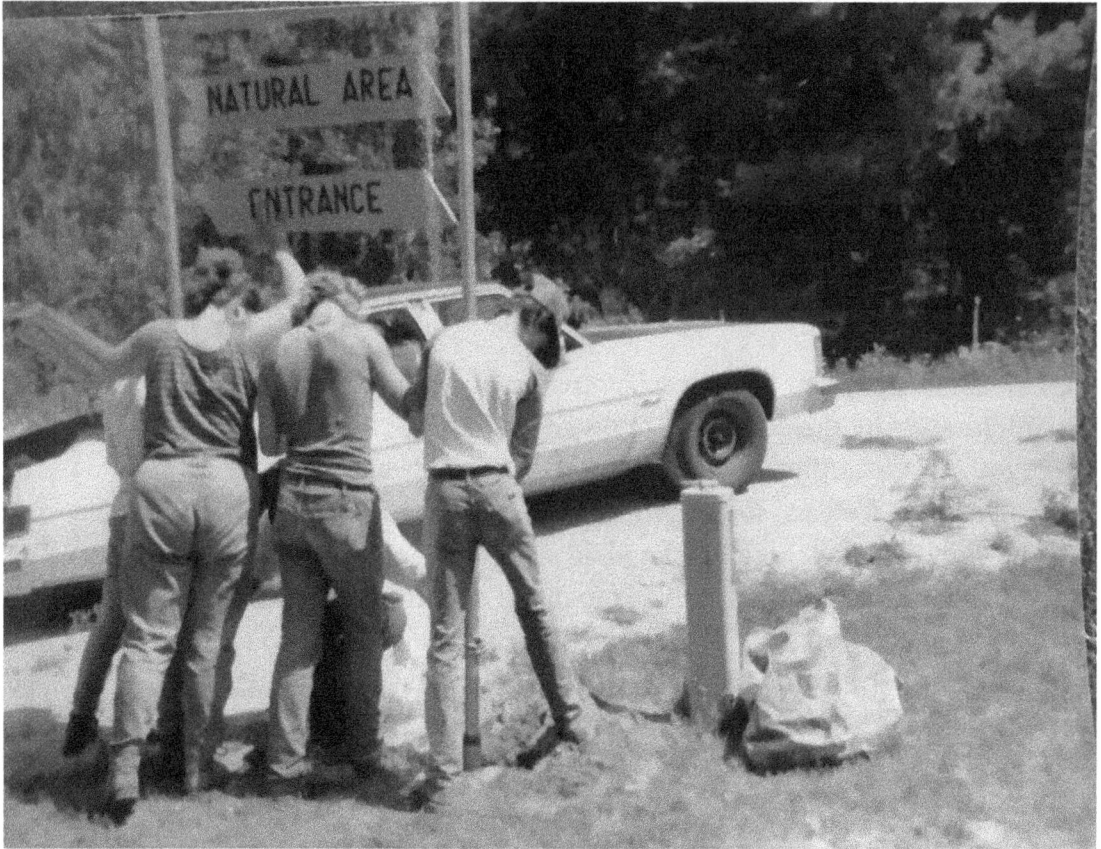

Original Grass River entrance sign – unknown volunteers

An initial grant from the Kresge Foundation of $30,000 enabled the first parcel to be purchased within the Grass River area. Later in 1976, the Kresge Foundation donated an additional $37,000. From there, the community rallied behind the project.

The initial grassroots fundraising committee spearheaded by Harold Beebe, Fred Dewitt, David Caldwell, Margaret Campbell, Harry Janis, Hellen & Walter O'Hair, and Warren Studley generated an additional $38,000 by the year 1976. Although there were many activists, Warren Studley is credited with the vision of this special area.

Some land was purchased by the Nature Conservancy (138 acres), some would be transferred from the MDNR (180 acres), and the rest (more than 700 acres)

would be bought from private landowners using federal grant dollars and private donations.

In 1977, the Nature Conservancy transferred its ownership to Antrim County.

A must-read for insight on the founding of the Grass River area is the book, *Uncommon Conservation – the Story of Saving Grass River*. I encourage you to visit the Grass River Natural Area and read about its acquisition.

The 1980s

After forty years of ownership, and a tremendous amount of effort devoted to forest management, the county forest lands were beginning to show the fruits of these efforts. Tree size and quality, a result of past treatments, enabled the county to increase the volume and quality of forest products sold from county forest lands.

The county continued to conduct forest stewardship activities on its properties in the 1980s. The cooperative extension agent, Burt Stanley, and the soil conservation service agent, Warren Studley, continued to be the facilitators for the agricultural and forestry committee.

Also, the county began to utilize foresters with the Conservation Districts and the MDNR to assist with the management and maintenance of county forest lands.

Attention to private land assistance, relative to forestry, began to take hold in the 1980s. The Department of Agriculture began to offer forestry assistance grants to local conservation districts. In 1984, Dave Johnson was hired to support private forestry activities in Antrim and Kalkaska Counties. Dave spent one year with the conservation district and was replaced by Tim Beyer in 1985.

Dave Johnson assisted the county with the marking and sale of pine products from Murphy Park. Here roughly 150 cords of pine were removed from the plantation. The county received $5,444.64 for the pine products. Later, Tim Beyer facilitated the thinning of pine from Skinkle Road, Simpson Road, and the Valley Road pine plantations—all generating income for the County.

Revenue from timber sales were deposited in the county's forestry fund established in the 1940s to maintain and manage the county forest properties. As this fund began to grow, the county was able to grant monies from this fund to other county entities. As an example, in 1987, the county utilized $3,000 to produce the plat book through 4H.

Additionally, the Antrim County Fair Board received $1,500 from the forestry fund. These funds were originally considered loans from the county but later the county waived the repayment of these dollars.

The county utilized the forestry fund as a loan fund for several other entities including Grass River, the conservation district, and others requesting temporary funds to complete a project.

An entire publication could be written on the private land programs initiated in the 1980s.

In 1983, a land trade was proposed by Grant Rowe from Shanty Creek. Mr. Rowe was interested in incorporating the forty acres on Frog Hollow Road into the Shanty Creek development. After much discussion, it was determined that the county was not able to trade the property without permission from the MDNR, given the deed restrictions placed on the parcel. The proposal was dropped.

The Elk River Chain of Lakes Watershed Project

Through the efforts of Warren Studley, USDA Soil Conservation Service agent, Antrim County's technical assistance to private landowners and the cost-sharing of stewardship practices were taken to the next level through a federal grant application in 1988.

A Watershed Plan and Assessment for the Elk River Watershed was developed by the Antrim and Charlevoix Conservation Districts, the Village of Bellaire, the Antrim County Commissioners, the USDA Soil Conservation Service, and the US Forest Service. It was submitted for funding under the federal Watershed Protection and Flood Prevention Act, Public Law 83-566.

WATERSHED PLAN
AND
ENVIRONMENTAL ASSESSMENT
FOR

ELK RIVER
WATERSHED

ANTRIM and CHARLEVOIX COUNTIES
MICHIGAN

WATERSHED PROTECTION

JULY 1988

The watershed project provided $2.5 million for technical assistance and land treatment on agricultural and forest lands within the Elk River Watershed from 1988–1998. In 1989, Mike Meriwether was hired by the Antrim Conservation District to administer ERW grant monies and provide technical assistance.

The Elk River Chain of Lakes Watershed was significant to Antrim County's

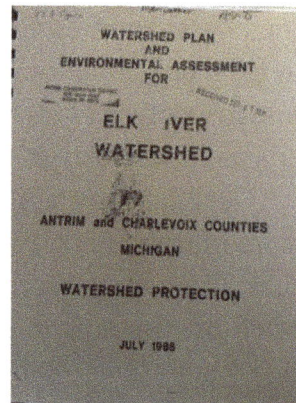

forestry program. It provided technical assistance dollars to assist private land-owners, the county, and other units of government for the next ten years.

Over this time period, 6,025 acres received forest land treatments. Among the many land treatment practices, tree planting was likely the most significant. 2,424,465 trees were planted in Antrim County during the ten-year project period.

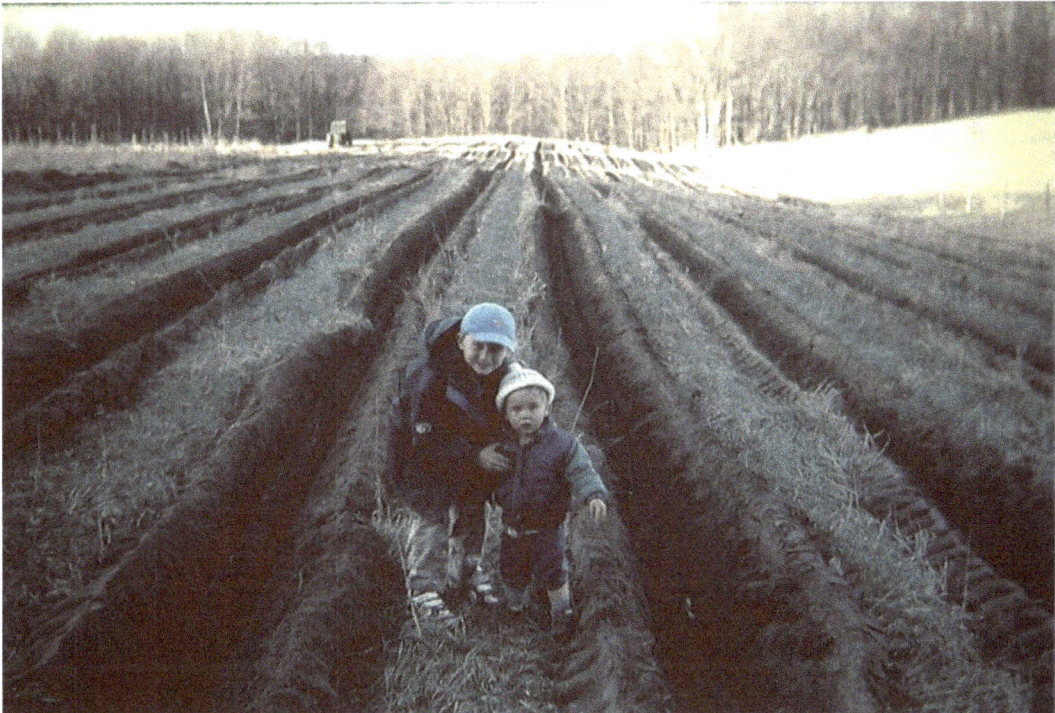

Gus and Gabe Meriwether, Elk River Watershed tree planting

The 1990s

Private forest land activities were the focus for the Antrim Conservation District forester in the 1990s. The county commissioners recognized the opportunity to utilize this program as a resource for its property management. The ACD forester was able to assist the county with the marking and sale of forest products from their properties. Other tree and property maintenance issues on county forest land were also being directed to the ACD forester.

On November 14, 1994, Antrim County and the Antrim Conservation District

entered into an agreement for the continued management and maintenance of county-owned properties.

At this time, the board of commissioners transferred responsibilities from the extension office to the ACD. The ACD forester was to: "advise the County Commissioners on forestry management of County lands on such matters but not limited to timber stand improvements, tree planting, harvesting, timber sales, management plans and other matters related to forestry management."

The forester would continue its private land obligations through the Elk River Watershed Grant and funding from the Michigan Department of Agriculture (MDA).

In 1990, Carl Eklund was hired under the MDA Forestry Assistance Program to service landowners in Kalkaska County, which allowed Antrim County to have a full-time forester focused on Antrim County and its landowners.

Gas And Oil Development

In the 1990s through 2008, the exploration and development of shallow Antrim gas resources began in the region, which included county forest lands. Through the deed transfer, the State of Michigan retained all the mineral rights to the county parcels. The state began to exercise its mineral options by leasing the gas development right, which included most county forest lands. While some parcels were leased as non-developmental, others were to receive wells and flow lines associated with the development of the natural gas resources.

Several of the county-owned properties were eligible for leasing and royalty payments. The prosecuting attorney and the forester negotiated lease payments and damages on these properties. Oil and gas revenue were deposited in an oil and gas fund created to accommodate these royalty payments to the county.

Antrim Gas Well

Although the county did not own the mineral rights on the municipal forest land acreages, and could not receive royalties, the forester was able to assess each development for surface damage payments. With a track record of forest management,

each well site and flow line were inventoried and an appraisal of the standing timber was recorded. Respective leasing companies were required to pay the assessed values of the timber resources destroyed during development.

Murphy Park and the Echo 31 parcels were among the first properties developed for gas production on county forests. Here the forester negotiated the relocation of the well site to minimize damage to the forest resources on the parcel.

The oil and gas companies were not conditioned or challenged to pay for timber products and often challenged the appraisals prepared by the forester. The prosecuting attorney, Charlie Koop, was prepared to litigate any opposition to compensating the county for its timber damages.

The forester argued that trees on county lands had received several thinnings and were growing higher quality trees. In addition, the conversion of these forest acres removed the future growth and development of the forest, further impacting the revenue expected from these acres.

As an example—on the Alba Road and M-66 parcel, DTE was required to pay $3,304.60 for the trees on the proposed well site. In addition, the forester required the gas company to cut and stack the wood products on-site. These products were then sold to local sawmills, allowing the county to capture these revenue as well.

Writing Surface Damage Reports

AN EXAMPLE

Prepared By Mike Meriwether, Forester Antrim Conservation District
Antrim County Forest Land — Del Mason Road Parcel

Custer Township: E ½, E ½, SE ¼, Section 16

Del Mason Road Parcel: 40 acres
The Del Mason Road parcel is an intensively managed northern hardwood forest.

Several intermediate treatments have occurred over the past twenty years. The treatments have been aimed at cultivating a forest environment capable of producing higher quality sawlog products on a sustainable basis.

A gas well and the corresponding flow line have been proposed for this parcel (by the Quicksilver Company). The disturbed well site has been estimated at 1.15 acres. The flow line easement extends to the east and is approximately 220 feet in length with an estimated width of 30 feet (0.15 acres).

All trees 10 inches in diameter measured at 4.5 feet above ground were recorded as sawlogs. Tree diameters were measured to the tenth of an inch. Merchantable height was estimated in 8-foot log segments. Corresponding tree volumes were calculated using tree diameter and merchantable height. The international ¼-inch tree scale was used for volume estimates within the standing timber. Trees were graded according to ocular estimates and recorded.

Ten year cutting rotations were used as a basis for calculating future values and lost opportunity due to the premature harvesting of trees. Three rotation cycles were calculated based on two inches of diameter growth rate per ten years with a twenty-inch maximum diameter.

The annual rate of return was set at 6.2%. The annual rate of return was based on a forty-six-year historical price trend study done by the North Central Forest Experimental Station, USDA Forest Service.

The economic loss to Antrim County is estimated at $5,576.56. It is recommended that Quicksilver Company submit this amount for the surface damages that will occur on the Del Mason Road parcel.

Revenue from the sale of timber, as well as surface damage payments from oil and gas development, were deposited in the county forestry fund. By October of 1997, the forestry fund balance was $149,600.

Antrim Creek Natural Area

In 1993, a large piece of the Lake Michigan shoreline in Banks Township went up for sale. The property was privately owned by the Jones Family. The property was 165 acres which contained nearly one mile of lake frontage. The Jones Family historically had allowed public ingress and egress to the lake shore for fishing, swimming, and picnicking. They also allowed Melvin Essenberg to give sand dune rides. Melvin had an International Scout with balloon tires and would charge for rides up and down the sand dunes on the property. Signage on 31 for "Mel's Sand Dune Rides" directed people to the property.

The Jones family contracted with Charlevoix Properties to develop the property and sell 35 +/- 100- to 200-foot lots along the Lake Michigan shoreline. It is noteworthy that Gary Strange from Charlevoix Properties quoted "the stakes were in the ground" and the property was prepared to be parceled out.

Glen Chown from the Grand Traverse Regional Land Conservancy (GTRLC) and Mark Stone, Antrim County Commissioner, recognized the value of this property and was able to convince the Jones Family as well as Burt Farbman and Gary Strange from Charlevoix Properties that this property could be better used as a public park or natural area. The Jones Family, Mr. Farbman, and Mr. Strange all agreed that this would be a possibility and were willing to put the development project on hold.

The next step was to get "buy-in" from Banks Township, the county, the State of Michigan, and the residents of the county. Gary Strange, Mark Stone, and the GTRLC spent the next three years working to secure funding and gathering public

support for the property acquisition. Monies to purchase the properties came from the Michigan Trust Fund, Antrim County, Banks Township, and public donations. Charlevoix Properties themselves donated $47,000 to the property acquisition.

With the local communities on board, funding from the trust fund and matching funds in place, the property was purchased by Antrim County from the Jones Family in 1996 for $4.3 million. The property is now the largest stretch of contiguous, undeveloped shoreline within the entire 132 miles of the bay coastline between Norwood and Northport.

The Antrim Creek Natural Area is governed by the county commissioners. The Antrim Creek Natural Area Commission was created through a 1996 endowment fund agreement between the county, Banks Township, the Grand Traverse Regional Land Conservancy, and the Grand Traverse Community Foundation. The commission is set up to assist the county in the management and maintenance of the property.

Friends of ACNA

"The mission of the Friends of the Antrim Creek Natural Area (ACNA) is to support the mission of the ACNA Commission which is: To manage the site as a natural area, to protect the diversity and fragile features found on the property and keep it accessible for recreational and educational use by the public."

The acquisition of the Antrim Creek Natural Area and several day park properties, along with the more recent additions to Grass River, have protected hundreds of acres within the county and are utilized by visitors and residents alike.

The 2000s

The Cedar River Natural Area

In 1998, a catastrophic storm event washed out several fairways on the newly constructed Cedar River Golf Course owned by Shanty Creek. Thousands of tons of sediment washed into the Cedar River impacting the riverbed, its banks, and fish populations. The Antrim Conservation District initiated some short- and long-term proposals to address the future restoration of the river. At the same time, the newly formed Friends of the Cedar River filed two lawsuits against Shanty Creek.

Abdeen Jabara, along with Russ Blasdale, can be credited with the formation of the Friends of the Cedar River. Mr. Jabara contributed $1,000 to hire an attorney and acted as the lead plaintiff in the lawsuit. He actively pursued Shanty Creek to hold them responsible for the damage done to the pristine river. The first case was to prevent Shanty Creek from utilizing the river water for snowmaking. The second case was limited to the repair and restoration of damages to the river caused by the golf course construction.

Through the court (Judge Powers) and with agreements from the Friends of the Cedar, Shanty Creek, and the Antrim Conservation District, a steering committee was established to facilitate the restoration of the river. Shanty Creek agreed to contribute $35,000 toward restoration projects. The Antrim Conservation District agreed to facilitate the restoration. This catastrophic event led to the acquisition discussions to protect the watershed in the long term.

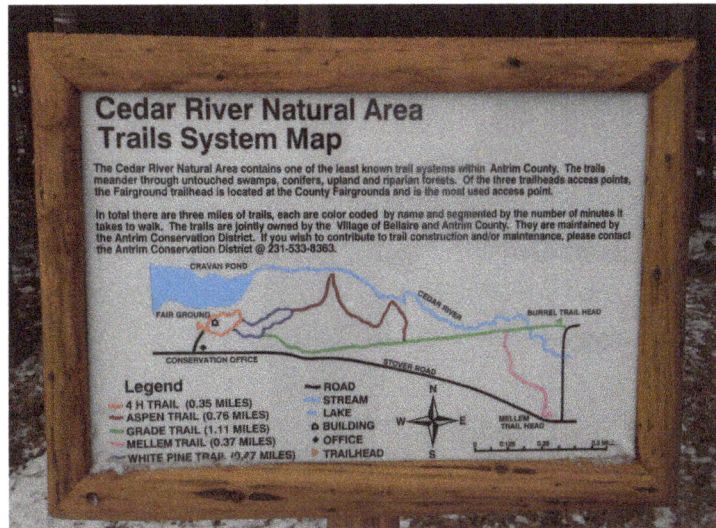

River Restoration

The ACD was able to leverage monies from Shanty Creek and donations from the private sector to acquire grant monies from the Michigan Clean Water Initiative, Inland Fisheries dollars, tribal donations, and other funds to address river restoration. In total $350,165 in grant monies were acquired. Local matching funds equaled $116,747. These monies were used to implement clean water projects, not only on the Cedar River but on the Rapid River as well.

In April of 2000, the ACD hired Cory Arsnoe to implement the work plan. Cory supervised the project with labor provided through the Camp Pugsley Correctional Facility. Cory and his crew installed erosion control structures, fish habitat structures, trails, bridges, and planted trees within the Cedar River Watershed and the Rapid River Watershed.

These activities were an important precursor to the establishment of the Cedar River Natural Area itself. With tremendous support from the Friends of the Cedar River, the Village of Bellaire, and riparian owners, protection of this watershed was now on the public radar.

In 2000, the ACD forester, Mike Meriwether, proposed that the county purchase the seventy-eight-acre Skaff property located east of Bellaire. The property contained pristine wetlands and river frontage. This parcel was also contiguous to the Village of Bellaire's property which included the Craven Park Campground, the ball fields, and the fairground.

Mike Meriwether and Janet Person negotiated the purchase of this property from the Skaff family. The Skaff family agreed to sell the property to the county for $135,000.

The question of how the property should be paid for became an issue. With support from the Village of Bellaire, the Grand Traverse Regional Land Conservancy

(GTRLC), the Friends of the Cedar River, and the conservation district, the county board of commissioners agreed to fund the purchase itself.

The county designated $95,000 from its Forestry Fund. The county also loaned $20,000 to the ACD with the expectation that they would partner with the GTRLC to repay the debt. In addition, $20,000 was raised from private donations.

It was agreed that a conservation easement would be placed on the property to protect it from future development.

This purchase set in motion the establishment of the Cedar River Natural Area.

A few years later in 2002, the county was able to expand the property by purchasing 109 acres from the Jabara Family. As a founding father of the Friends of the Cedar River, Abdeen Jabara was extremely interested in protecting the natural beauty of this property and was willing to sell it to the county at a reduced rate. Mr. Jabara offered to sell the property at 25% less than the appraised value. The property appraisal was $357,000, constituting an $89,250 donation from the Jabara Family. The county utilized the Michigan Natural Resources Trust Fund, and with assistance from the GTRLC, purchased the property from Mr. Jabara and created the Cedar River Natural Area.

The creation of the Cedar River Natural Area is another example of the community coming together to protect property and natural resources by adding the property to the county land inventories.

The natural area now includes land owned by the Village of Bellaire and the consolidated county lands.

The management and maintenance responsibilities were given to the Antrim Conservation District's forestry program. Placing the Cedar River Natural Area

under the supervision of the ACD Forestry Program allowed the county and ACD access to forestry revenue for recreational and conservation improvements on this parcel plus several other county-owned properties.

> It was moved by Crawford, seconded by McLeod that the Cedar River Natural Area be placed under the direction of the County Lands, Agriculture, and Forestry Committee with the management by the County Forester. Motion carried all members present voting yes.

Forestry Fund revenue were used to improve fish habitats, improve and expand trail networks within the natural area, and reconstruct the old train bridge crossing the Cedar River near Burrell Road. In 2017, the Boucher family donated 163 acres along the Cedar River to the Antrim Conservation District. Although not contiguous to the existing natural area, these acres are considered to be part of the Cedar River Natural Area and are maintained by the ACD.

Glacial Hills Pathway and Natural Area

One of the most recent land acquisitions and consolidation of forest-land properties is the Glacial Hills Pathway and Natural Area. This property consists of a total of 784 acres of forested uplands. County community forest lands made up the basis for this recreational area. 418 acres have been historically owned and managed for forestry purposes by Antrim County.

Through a collaborative effort with Forest Home Township, the Grand Traverse Regional Land Conservancy, the Village of Bellaire, the Olsen Foundation, and the county, a larger contiguous block of public property was pieced together.

Through the Michigan Natural Resources Trust fund, Forest Home Township was able to acquire 177 acres. The trust fund also provided matching funds to Antrim County for the purchase of 169 acres consolidating its ownerships in Sections 13, 14, and 23 within Forest Home Township.

It is noteworthy that matching funds ($178,000) utilized to purchase the Glacial Hills property were from revenue generated through the sale of timber from county forest lands.

The Glacial Hills Pathway and Natural Area provides thirty-one miles of

mountain biking and hiking trails. Forest management mixed with the recreational use of this property is a relatively unique example of multiple-use property ownership.

The pathway itself is managed and maintained by the Friends of Glacial Hills, a nonprofit group supported by volunteers and public donations. Forestry and natural resource management practices are provided through the Antrim Conservation District forester, which has oversight responsibilities for this property through the cooperative agreement with the county.

The county now had over sixty years of commitment to their forest land acreages. They were also seeing increased revenue from the sale of timber. These revenue savings allowed the county to build on its land holdings and fund park and community projects without using tax revenue.

PROTECTING FOREST LANDS

Who knew that protecting our forest lands from exchange, sale, or conversion would be a subject for discussion? Once these lands were acquired, pressures to develop, sell, trade, or convert them began almost immediately.

As far back as the 1940s, proposals and discussions took place regarding the usage of these parcels. The State of Michigan was consistent in reminding the county what these lands were to be utilized for. Some properties were lost, and some alternative uses were granted on several properties. Several land protection tools have been put in place to protect the unique values of the county lands.

Conservation Easements

A conservation easement is a voluntary, legal agreement that permanently limits the uses of the land to protect its conservation values. Also known as a conservation restriction or conservation agreement, a conservation easement is one option to protect property for future generations.

Antrim County owns several properties that are protected through a conservation easement. They include Antrim Creek Natural Area, the Cedar River Natural Area, Glacial Hills Natural Area, and portions of the Grass River Natural Area.

Conservation easements have been used to protect private lands from development as well. The Grand Traverse Regional Land Conservancy administers several thousand acres of easement-protected properties in the County.

Reverter Clause

The transfer of forestry property deeds did not come free and clear. The State of Michigan retains ownership of all mineral rights. In addition, the state placed a reversionary clause on the parcels that reads, "It is expressly understood that the lands herein described will be used solely for forestry purposes and when same ceases to be used for such purposes, it shall revert to the State of Michigan."

This deed restriction proved to be a valuable tool in protecting county properties. Many attempts to trade, sell, or convert these properties to other uses were proposed over the past eighty-seven years.

In 2006, the state legislature passed Act 179 of PA 2006, Relinquishment of Reverter on Municipal Forest Deeds, allowing schools and municipalities to remove the reverter rights from some deed-restricted properties. The prosecutor, Charlie Koop, recommended the county board of commissioners discuss the pros and cons of removing this deed restriction from specific deeds.

The Antrim Conservation District forester, Mike Meriwether, argued that removing these deed restrictions could, and most likely would, jeopardize these parcels making them subject to sale, trade, and or conversion at the whim of future politics.

The ACD forester was asked to prepare the property descriptions and application, and submit it to the MDNR.

In 2010, the MDNR approved the application to remove the reverter clause from fifteen parcels owned by Antrim County. Properties over 121 acres in size or those parcels with access to water did not qualify for the removal of this clause. See Table 2.

Forest Property Area Ordinance

All forest lands acquired under the Municipal Forest Program have been protected through the Antrim County Forestry Ordinance passed in 2009. To protect these

properties, a Forestry Property Area Ordinance was proposed and drafted by Mr. Koop. Antrim County Ordinance #1 of 2009 was adopted through a unanimous vote of the board of commissioners. In short, the ordinance required a vote of the people as well as a 3/5 majority vote of the electors voting thereon to sell, exchange, lease, or place liens on county forest lands. See Table 2.

Township	Forest Name	Acreage	Restricted By
Kearney	Pete Wilks Forest	98.4 acres	Ordinance
Kearney	Dickerson Road	90 acres	Deed, ordinance
Echo	Dickerson Road	160 acres	Deed, ordinance
Kearney	Batchelder Road	40 acres	Ordinance
Kearney	Cedar River Natural Area	192 acres	Conservation Easement
Forest Home	Govt. Lot 7 (Mohrmann)	45.70 acres	Deed, ordinance
Forest Home	Govt. Lot 6 (Mohrmann)	12 acres	Deed, ordinance
Central Lake	Intermediate Lake	48 acres	Deed, ordinance
Star	Star	40 acres	Ordinance
Star	Lake of the North	20 acres	Ordinance
Star	Lake of the North	40 acres	Ordinance
Custer	Leonard Road	80 acres	Ordinance
Custer	Frog Hollow	40 acres	Ordinance
Custer	Del Mason Road	40 acres	Ordinance
Custer	Simpson Road	160 acres	Deed, ordinance
Custer	Lake of the Woods	40 acres	Deed, ordinance
Forest Home	Vandermark	68 acres	Ordinance, easement
Forest Home	Vandermark	10 acres	Ordinance, easement
Forest Home	Orchard Hill	20 acres	Ordinance, easement

Forest Home	Glacial Hills	180 acres	Ordinance, easement
Forest Home	Vandermark	20 acres	Ordinance, easement
Forest Home	Kirkpatrick Forest	320 acres	Deed, ordinance
Echo	Intermediate River	40 acres	Deed, ordinance
Echo	Intermediate River	40 acres	Deed, ordinance
Central Lake	Muckle Road	80 acres	Deed, ordinance
Echo	Dickerson Road	160 acres	Deed, ordinance
Echo	Murphy Park	76 acres	Ordinance
Echo	Lewis Road	80 acres	Ordinance
Echo	Skinkle Road	160 acres	Deed, ordinance
Mancelona	Valley Road	40 acres	Ordinance
Mancelona	Hawk Lake	160 acres	Deed, ordinance
Torch Lake	Barnes Park	82 acres	Deed, ordinance
Torch Like	Barnes Park	10 acres	Deed, ordinance
Torch Lake	Barnes Park	10 acres	Deed, ordinance
Banks	Lore Road	40 acres	Ordinance
Chestonia	Alba Road	74.70 acres	Deed, ordinance
Chestonia	Alba Road	20 acres	Deed, ordinance
Chestonia	Alba Road	80 acres	Deed, ordinance
Central Lake	Prince Property	20 acres	Ordinance
Morris Road	Jordan	120 acres	Deed, ordinance

Table 2: Municipal Forest Deed Information

FINANCING FOREST LANDS

Forest Revenue and Expenses

Revenue generated through the sale of forest products are deposited in the county's forestry fund.

Common expenditures include periodic land surveys, road and trail construction and maintenance, gates, signage, non-commercial thinning, tree planting, and wildlife habitat improvements. The forestry fund has also been instrumental in the acquisition of many of our parks and natural areas. The sale of forest products has provided revenue that were used to purchase properties or as matching grant funding.

Today, revenue far outpace the expenses of maintaining the county's forest lands. Surplus revenue are being used to supplement parks and recreation within the county.

County forest lands represent a sizable land asset for the county and an equally sizable forest reserve for future revenue.

> The sale of forest products has provided revenue that were used to purchase properties or as matching grant funding.

Sustainable forest management practices are aimed at increasing forest revenue, while at the same time, providing educational and recreational opportunities for residents and visitors.

Forestry Fund

At the beginning of 1940, the forestry fund was set up to accommodate tree planting expenses and revenue from the sale of firewood as well as a few timber sales. The administration of these transactions was through the Michigan State University Extension Agent with oversight from the county's Agricultural and Forestry Committee.

The exponential growth of this fund did not occur until the 1990s, when higher valued products began to be sold from county lands.

In 2022, the forestry fund balance was $350,000 +/-. This fund represents more than eighty years of responsible forest management and savings by our county commissioners.

The forestry fund has remained a significant source of funding for many county projects, specifically land acquisitions. Although the county commissioners sometimes view these dollars as general fund monies, they have historically utilized them for conservation purposes. Keep in mind that the revenue placed in this fund are from the sale of forest products from county-owned lands, which have enabled the county to fund conservation projects without raising taxes for this specific purpose.

Historical Revenue Sharing

Throughout the 2000s, the State of Michigan struggled with the funding of private land services. Technical service grants were beginning to be an unstable source of funding for the conservation districts. In 2007, the state discontinued funding for private forestry services. Both the Antrim Conservation District and the county recognized the value of having a full-time forester working with private land ownerships and county lands.

In 2006, a revenue-sharing memorandum of understanding was developed and approved by the county commissioners. This was a way to provide funding to the Antrim Conservation District for the purpose of providing forestry technical assistance to private owners while still maintaining their properties. The MOU called for 75% of forest revenue to be utilized by the ACD to employ a forester. The remaining 25% of forest revenue would be deposited in the existing forestry fund.

The agreement provided for continued assistance to private landowners, schools, and local governments.

While this agreement was a creative way to fund a forestry position in the county, it did have its limitations. Most significantly, the sale of timber from county lands fluctuated from year to year. Timber sales were historically based on forest management needs, markets, and other factors. Generating income to support a forestry program had the potential to run counter with forest management itself. While our county forests could generate enough revenue to support a forestry program in the short term, it possibly put the forester in a position of conflict with the actual long-term needs of the forests.

In 2009, the ACD and the county commissioners reconstructed the MOU. The county supported funding a forestry position through the ACD from its general fund. It agreed to support the management and maintenance costs of its municipal forests through the existing forestry fund. Stabilizing the forestry program enabled the ACD forester to spend more time on county-wide stewardship activities within the community.

These activities included:

- The acquisition of state and federal dollars for work on the Jordan River Road;
- The securing of U.S. EPA 319 grant dollars—federal monies—dedicated to clean water activities;
- Matching funds provided through the county forestry fund were used to complete fishery improvements within the Cedar River Natural Area;
- Forestry monies were used for trail improvements and bridge construction within the Cedar River Natural Area;
- In 2003, the ACD reconstructed the railroad bridge, on the Jabara Property, within the Cedar River Natural Area;
- It allowed for the construction of many trail networks.

Selling Standing Timber—Timber Harvesting

In some ways, timber harvesting, conducted on county forest lands, constitutes the end product of long-term forest management. Significantly, Antrim County has allowed the forest management on their properties to occur without outside

pressures to generate income. The harvesting of trees is an important component of forest management itself.

Today, most of the wood products sold from county-owned forest properties are done through the competitive bidding process. To do this, the forester marks and records the number of trees, tree volumes, and other considerations regarding the harvest of trees. The selected trees are then offered to the forest products industry. An industry representative is required to view the selected trees and place a lump sum "bid" on the trees.

On occasion, the county forester will request that wood products be sold on a cut-and-scale basis. The products are selected or identified to be harvested by area, then the forester will negotiate the sale of these trees to an industry representative. This can be done when volumes or values are not significant enough to attract competitive bids. A cut-and-scale sale may also be initiated when specific products are to be marketed where limited markets of producers exist.

In 2022, Antrim County sold $165,265 of wood products from its forest properties.

A cutting timeline for harvesting has been developed within the planning process. (See Table 3.) It is understood that the timeline for when and where to cut often considers market trends and damaging agents such as insects, diseases, and weather events.

In 2022, Antrim County sold $165,265 of wood products from its forest properties.

It should be noted that not all county forest lands can sustain this type of forest return, but many can. Properties not capable of producing income are valued for their recreational usage, wetland protection, and other community or environmental benefits.

Parcel	Last Harvest	Projected Harvest	Acreage	Notes
Alba Road	2012	2023	100	
Alba Road	2018	2028	40	Bundy Hill
Dickerson Road	2010	2024	120	West
Dickerson Road	2023	2035	130	
Frog Hollow	2008	2024	40	
Glacial Hills	2016	2024	60	Bedell 60
Lewis Road	2006	2024	80	
Lake of North	2020	2030	60	2 parcels
Morhmann	2009	2023	80	Muckle Rd
Morhmann	1997	2023	20	
Morris Road	2020	2030	120	
Wilks Forest	2023	2033	100	
Simpson Road	2013	2023	160	
Star 40	2013	2023	40	
Valley Road	2008	2023	40	
Delmason	2014	2024	40	
Barnes Park	2014	2024	40	
Kirkpatrick	2014	2025	320	
Leonard Road	2017	2027	80	
Prince	2017	2027	20	
Lake of Woods	2013	2024	40	
Hawk Lake	2020	2024	100	Pine
Batchelder	2000	2024	40	

Table 3: 2023 Harvest Schedule

PROVIDING FOREST MANAGEMENT SERVICES

Conducting property inventories, developing forest management plans, planting trees, harvesting trees, and managing forest resources on county-owned forest lands became a higher priority starting in 1994 when the county contracted with the Antrim Conservation District to facilitate the management and maintenance of county-owned forest lands. This agreement continues to the present day (2024). Although some non-commercial improvement cutting was undertaken, most of the timber harvesting projects were conducted for the commercial sale of forest products.

Administration

Under the Municipal (community) Forestry Act, the state recommended a forestry commission be set up by local municipalities receiving properties. The commission was to oversee land use and forestry activities. There are no records of an actual commission being established in Antrim County.

In Antrim County, the Board of Supervisors of Antrim County (now the Board of Commissioners) established the Antrim County

Agricultural and Forestry Committee. This committee was responsible for the initial forest management activities that took place on many forest lands. Records indicate that Albert Barns was the first chairperson of the Agricultural and Forestry Committee under the board of supervisors around 1939.

The Agricultural and Forestry Committee was made up of elected officials and appointed representatives from the community. In 2000, the committee's name was changed to the Parks and Forestry Committee.

This committee was a function of the Antrim County Board of Commissioners. It was able to gather information, receive public comment, and recommend actions to the Antrim County Board of Supervisors / Commissioners. Forestry activities within this committee were discussed frequently.

The committee structure within the Antrim County Board of Commissioners was disbanded in 2019.

Today, forest lands and other properties are administered through a cooperative agreement between the Antrim Conservation District and the Antrim County Commissioners. Oversight is provided by the Antrim County Board of Commissioners.

Antrim Conservation District Forester

Through its cooperative agreement with Antrim County, the Antrim Conservation District hired a forester to oversee county land activities and provide technical support to the county, local governments, nonprofit groups, and private landowners. The responsibilities of the county forester are as follows:

- Write and maintain forest management plans for individual parcels
- Implement forest management plans
- Monitor the use of Antrim County Forest Lands
- Maintain property lines
- Assist the Antrim County Board of Commissioners with special projects
- Oversee all timbering and improvement cutting
- Maintain designated recreational trails
- Improve recreational usage where appropriate
- Issue firewood cutting permits
- Report annually to the Antrim County Board of Commissioners

- Provide technical services to private landowners, schools, groups, and units of government

Antrim County Forestry Program

VISION
To maintain healthy, vibrant, and productive forests within Antrim County.

MISSION
To manage public properties and provide technical assistance to non-industrial private forest lands, so they are sustainable far into the future.

GOALS
- Protecting unique features
- Ensuring sustainable forests in Antrim County
- To protect open space
- To provide recreational opportunities
- Demonstrate sustainable forest management
- Generate revenue within the community

BENEFITS
- Providing habitat for wildlife
- Increasing overall site productivity
- Increasing wood production
- Forestry education for the public
- Restoring forest ecology
- Improved biological diversity

OBJECTIVES (MEASURABLE)
PUBLIC LANDS
- Acquire public forest lands where practical
- Consolidate public forest lands into manageable units
- Develop forest management plans for county-owned forest lands

- Manage public forest lands, so they are sustainable
- Demonstrate sustainable forestry practices

PRIVATE LANDS
- Assist with forest management planning on private forest lands
- Assist private forest landowners with specific management activities
- Assist local governments, schools, and groups
- Educate the public

Managing Community Forest Lands

Today the county forester has taken a "close to nature" approach to managing and maintaining many of our county-owned forest lands. This concept uses natural processes to fulfill specific management goals. This approach represents a divergence from historical forest-management practice and is aimed at achieving the following goals:

- Ensuring sustainable county forests far into the future
- Restoring forest ecology
- Improving biological diversity
- Protecting unique features
- Providing for wildlife
- Increased site productivity overall
- Increasing wood production

Each "forest type" has its own unique characteristics. Many of our county forests contain multiple forest types, which are managed individually. Some of the major forest types are described in Table 4. We use common names rather than scientific names because these are the names used by foresters and landowners. The Michigan Natural Features Inventory (MNFI) has identified and described natural communities in Michigan.

Common Name	Scientific Name	Number of Acres	Percentage
Northern Hardwood Forests	Mesic Northern Forest	1,803.64	59%
Aspen Stands	Aspen Stands found in Mesic Northern Forest	118.27	3.9%
Oak Forests	Dry-mesic Northern Forest	177.40	5.8%
Northern Conifer Swamps	Rich Conifer Swamp	473.09	15.5%
Other Wetland Types includes marshlands, lowland hardwoods, riparian forests		79.14	2.6%
Pine Plantations		295.68	9.7%
Miscellaneous Stands of spruce, jack pine, white pine and other smaller acreages		109.56	3.5%
TOTAL		3,056.8	100%

Table 4: Community Forest Types

Northern Hardwood Forests

The northern hardwood forest represents 59% or roughly 1,803.64 acres of the municipal forest lands owned by the county. The northern hardwood forest also represents the highest economic potential of all the forest types.

Northern hardwood forests are the dominant forest type here in Antrim County. Sugar maple, beech, and basswood are considered the climax forest species. Often white ash, red maple, hemlock, and yellow birch are components. Black cherry, red oak, iron wood, and aspen also can be found within this forest type.

Northern hardwood forests can be managed for several objectives including higher-valued lumber products, watershed protection, wildlife, recreation, or any combination of these.

Historical practices of diameter-limit cuts, single species removal, and high-grade harvesting have decimated most of our natural hardwood forest here in Michigan. Diameter limit cuts have ruined stand structure, and removals by species—as well as invasive insects and diseases—have destroyed diversity within our forest ecosystems. High-grading practices have removed genetically superior trees and left poor quality trees behind to propagate the next generation of forest.

Restoring the forest ecology of the northern hardwood forests owned by the county is the primary focus of the forest management activities taking place on our county forest lands.

The long-range management goals for the county's northern hardwood forests

are aimed at encouraging and quickly developing a size class distribution capable of producing sustainable yields of high-quality hardwood products in conjunction with other ecological benefits into the future.

Some specific management objectives for the northern hardwood forest are as follows:

- Improve tree recruitment in seedling and sapling classes
- Improve tree growth
- Improve tree height and form
- Favor genetically superior trees
- Maintain and increase wildlife habitats (all species)

The Pete Wilks Forest and the Alba Road Forest are excellent examples where periodic thinning has encouraged a "close to nature" management approach.

Aspen Stands

Individual stands of aspen represent approximately 4% of our county forest lands. Although not abundant within the county's ownership, the aspen component within several parcels is significant to many wildlife populations. Roughly sixty-five acres have been intensively managed with the goal of maintaining the aspen component.

Aspen stands are valuable for several reasons. Although the principal use of aspen is for manufacturing paper and particleboard, it is also an important source of food and shelter for many forms of wildlife including deer, woodcock, grouse, and wild turkey. A multitude of songbirds also rely on aspen forests. Aspen is considered an intolerant species that is unable to grow and establish properly under its own shade or the shade of its associates.

Aspen is maintained and managed primarily for wildlife purposes on county forest lands. Some income is realized from the management of the aspen forests on our county lands.

Examples of aspen being maintained for wildlife purposes can be seen at our Lake of the North properties and the Pete Wilks Forest area.

Aspen forest

Oak Forests

The county owns several parcels that have been devoted to the management and maintenance of red oak within the northern hardwood forest types. Although oak exists as a small component within many of the larger northern hardwood forest areas, there are several parcels that contain a higher percentage of red oak and are considered "oak forests."

Oaks can be maintained and managed for higher valued forest products. They are also significant to wildlife and can be a valuable source of food, shelter, and nesting habitats for a wide range of wildlife species.

There are three parcels that contain enough oak to be considered an oak forest. They include Barnes Park Forest, Lake of the Woods, and the Frog Hollow forests.

Northern Conifer Swamp

A small percentage of the county-owned forest lands contain northern conifer swamps. These forests include white cedar, hemlock, and balsam fir. Other associated species can include tamarack, yellow birch, black ash, white pine, and red maple.

This forest type is typically found within riparian areas—along streams or lake shores. Generally, these areas are low in forest product values and high in other environmental attributes.

Our Intermediate River Forest, the Cedar River Natural Area, Grass River Natural Area, and the Mohrmann Park Forest contain examples of the valued northern conifer swamp.

Other Wetland Types

There are other wetland types represented on our county lands, but not all of them are forested. They are critically important for watershed and wetland protection, as well as wildlife and fish habitat. Generally, these areas are not considered significant from a forest-management standpoint. The county has protected these lands as natural areas for the public's enjoyment and passive recreation such as bird-watching, hiking, and cross-country skiing.

These wetland communities include marshes, wet meadows, fens, wooded dune-swale complex, and wetland complexes. They are managed to maintain natural ecosystems, processes, and native species diversity.

Examples of these wetland types can be found in the Antrim Creek Natural Area, Cedar River Natural Area, and Grass River Natural Area.

Red Pine Plantations

Red pine plantations represent approximately 10% of the county-owned forest lands. Red pine plantations were established from the 1940s to the 1960s. They have been managed intensively to produce lumber products. Periodic thinning has created an environment where hardwood regeneration is occurring in the understory of many of these plantations.

Many of the county-owned pine plantations are now in their third and fourth cutting rotations. This means they have been thinned several times.

Red pine is shade intolerant and long-lived. Some stands live for two hundred years, and some individual trees can survive four hundred years. In commercial rotations, maximum ages are 60–120 years. Although it is possible to grow red pine in either even-aged or uneven-aged stands, even-aged plantations give better results, because red pine grows best in full sunlight.

Most of the red pine plantations on county lands have reached a point where the forester will have to decide to remove the remaining red pine trees and re-plant to establish new trees or allow these areas to convert to northern hardwood forests through natural succession.

Examples of red pine plantation management can be seen at our Hawk Lake and Simpson Road properties.

COMMUNITY (Municipal) FOREST AREAS

The Antrim Conservation District Forester has classified forty parcels containing 3,056.8 acres of public property as managed community forest parcels (Table 5).

The county forester consolidated contiguous parcels into twenty-six community forest areas. Management plans have been developed for each area.

These forest lands include properties acquired under Michigan's Community Forest Act as well as purchased properties, donated lands, and/or lands otherwise designated as Antrim County Forests by the county board of commissioners.

In addition, managed forest areas can generate revenue through the sale of forest products. Forest revenue have been used to maintain the properties and utilized to match funds for land acquisition grants. Glacial Hills, the Cedar River Natural Area, Antrim Creek Natural Area, and the Grass River Natural Area have all utilized revenue generated from the sale of forest products created by our county forest lands.

Those properties classified as Antrim County Community Forest Lands are considered public assets and have been protected from use, conversion, or sale through conservation easements, reversionary deed restrictions, ordinances, and other agreements entered by the county. It has been the intent of the county commissioners, both past and present, to protect and utilize these properties for future generations to enjoy.

Our county-owned forest lands are scattered throughout Antrim County, with most being easily accessible from county roads. The Kirkpatrick Forest Area, combined with the Glacial Hills parcels, represents the largest contiguous acreage at 607 acres. The average size of the county forest parcel is seventy-seven acres.

Antrim County Forest Areas (28)	Township	Section	Year Acquired	Acreage
Alba Road and M66 Forest Area	Chestonia	28,29	1940	175.0
Antrim Creek Natural Area	Banks		1996	165.0
Barnes Park Forest Area	Torch Lake	1	1939	156.74
Batchelder Road Forest Area	Kearney	29	1966	40.0
Cedar River Natural Area & Forest Area	Kearney	20,21	2000	233.0
Del Mason Road Forest Area	Custer	16	1950	40.0
Dickerson Road Forest Area	Echo	31	1950	250.0
Echo Township Section 31 Forest Area				
Fred Prince Forest Area	Central Lake	34	2014	20.0
Frog Hollow Forest Area	Custer	4	1952	40.0
Glacial Hills Pathway and Natural Area & Forest Area	Forest Home	14,23	1950	288.0
Grass River Natural Area	Custer, Forest Home & Helena			1492.0
Hawk Lake Forest Area	Mancelona	16	1935	160.0
Intermediate River Forest Area	Echo	27	1940	40.0
Lake of the Woods Forest Area	Custer	17	1940	40.0

Antrim County Forest Areas (28)	Township	Section	Year Acquired	Acreage
Lake of the North 40 Forest Area	Star	26	1952	40.0
Lake of the North 20 Forest Area	Star	27	1952	20.0
Leonard Road Forest Area	Custer	28	1950	80.0
Lewis Road Forest Area	Echo	24	1950	80.0
Lore Road Forest Area	Banks	36	1950	40.0
Mohrmann Park Natural Area & Forest Area	Forest Home	1	1940	187.5
Morris Road Forest Area	Jordan	27	1950	120.0
Murphy Park Forest Area	Echo	28	1951	73.0
Pete Wilks Forest Area	Kearney	8	1950	98.4
Simpson Road Forest Area	Custer	12	1950	160.0
Skinkle Road Forest Area	Echo	34	1950	160.0
Star Township 40 Forest Area	Star	10	1952	40.0
Valley Road Forest Area	Mancelona	15	1951	41.0
Walter Kirkpatrick Forest Area	Forest Home	13	1950	320.0

Table 5: Antrim County Community Forest Areas

Alba Road and M-66 Forest Area

The Alba Road and M-66 Forest Area is 175 acres of northern hardwood forest consisting of rolling terrain with a few steep slopes. Access to this area is from the Alba Highway, which borders the north side of the property and M-66, and bisects some of the property. Logging roads exist on the parcel and are frequently used by hunters, hikers, snowmobiles, and other motorized vehicles.

The Alba Road and M-66 Forest Area is an actively managed northern hardwood forest where trees are harvested periodically for forest products, wildlife habitat, trail construction or maintenance, insect and disease control, or a combination of all of these. This area has been leased for oil and gas development.

Organized commercial forest management activities began in 1994, and have generated $286,497.10 in revenue through the sale of forest products.

The parcel is contiguous to the state-owned Mackinaw State Forest, which lies to the north and includes the Jordan River Watershed.

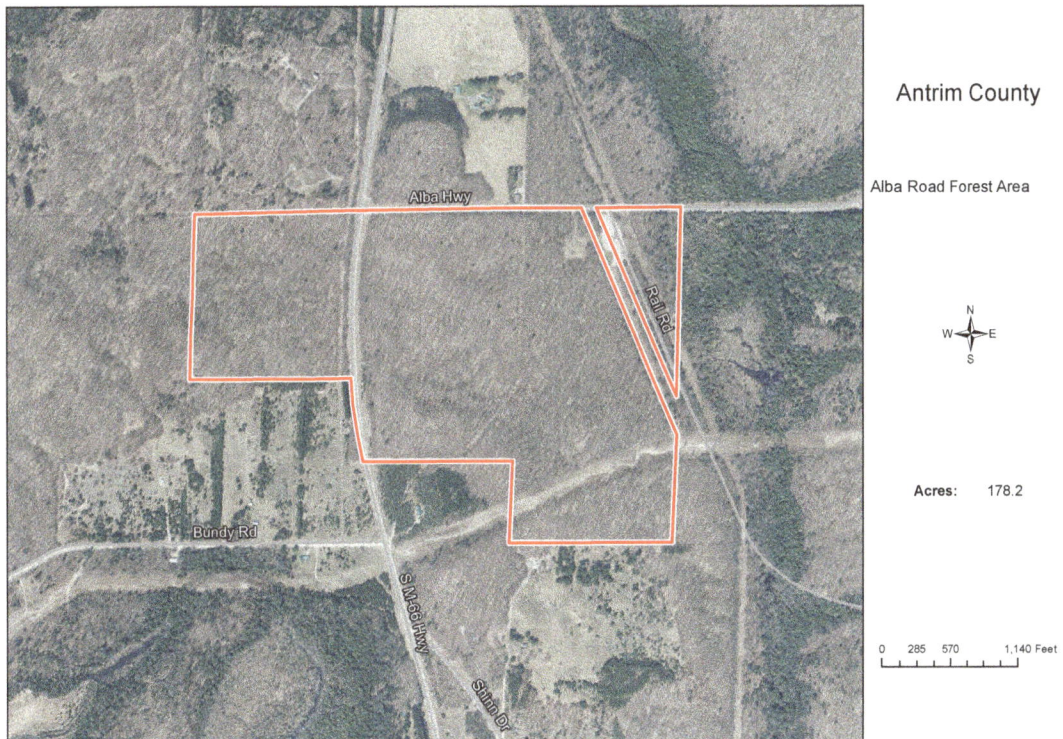

Antrim County

Alba Road Forest Area

Acres: 178.2

0 285 570 1,140 Feet

Notes:
The Alba Road Forest Area can be accessed from M66 and or Alba Road. It contains several multiple use trails.

Map Produced by
Antrim County Equalization
March 2023

UNIQUE FEATURES

- Example of uneven aged hardwood forest
- Example of black cherry management within the Northern Hardwood Forest
- Unimproved drive-through access
- Contains multiple unimproved logging roads for hiking and walking

ALBA ROAD—A SUCCESS STORY

It is important to document the power of forest management by example. The Alba Road and M-66 parcel can provide some insight into this value.

From the years 1994 through 2018, there were six timber sales conducted on the parcel. The 175 acres were divided into several management units with forest management needs individually addressed. Collectively, there were 2,576 trees harvested, totaling 415,956 board feet of lumber products.

There were also several stand improvement cuttings where firewood was sold. The county received $257,497.10 in stumpage payment for these products.

Additional revenue came from oil and gas surface damage payments ($5,000) and power line easement payments ($24,000).

Barnes Park Forest Area

The Barnes Park Forest Area is 156.74 acres of pine forest, northern hardwood forest, aspen forest, oak forest, and wetland complexes. It consists of flat terrain with a few short slopes. This area is contiguous to the Barnes Park Campground and can be accessed from the park. Several improved walking trails loop through this forest area which are frequently used by campers, hikers, and cross-country skiers.

The Barnes Park Forest Area is an actively managed forest, where trees are harvested periodically for forest products, wildlife habitat, trail construction or maintenance, insect and disease control, or a combination of all of these. The most recent harvesting of trees occurred in 2006. Here the red pine plantation was thinned. In addition, harvesting included the development of a trail system for visitors, as well as aspen and oak management.

Organized commercial forest-management activities began in 1994, and they have generated $29,000.00 in revenue through the sale of forest products.

UNIQUE FEATURES

- Example of oak forest
- Example of aspen management
- Examples of white pine and natural pine management
- Red pine plantation management
- Forestry interpretative signage
- Contiguous to campground area

Antrim County

Barnes Park Forest Area

Acres: 102

0   335   670   1,340 Feet

Notes:
The Barnes Park Forest Area adjoins the Barnes Park Campground. It has several forest interpretive walking trails available to the public. Also used in winter for cross country skiing.

Map Produced by:
Antrim County Equalization
March 2023

Batchelder Road Forest Area

Ownership of the Batchelder Road Forest was transferred from the Village of Bellaire to Antrim County in 1966. It has been included and maintained as county forest land.

The Batchelder Forest Area is a forty-acre parcel located west of Bellaire. It can be accessed from Batchelder Road off Stover Road. The forest consists of northern hardwood forest with larger diameter aspen as a component. The large aspen are retained for wildlife purposes. A pine plantation was planted on the property for erosion control purposes.

Hunters and hikers extensively use the Batchelder Forest Area. There is a horse trail that bisects the property, which is used by neighboring property owners.

UNIQUE FEATURES

- Older-growth aspen have been retained on the property for wildlife purposes

Antrim County

Batchelder Road Forest

Acres: 40

0   120   240   480 Feet

Notes:
The Batchelder Road Forest is accessed from Batchelder Road off of Stover Road.

Map Produced by:
Antrim County Equalization
March 2023

Del Mason Forest Area

The Del Mason Forest Area is a forty-acre parcel located at the corner of Alden Highway and Del Mason Road with access from Del Mason Road. It contains high-quality northern hardwood forest and is situated on flat terrain. Logging roads exist on the parcel and are frequently used by hunters and hikers.

The Del Mason Forest Area is an actively managed northern hardwood forest, where trees are periodically harvested for forest products, wildlife habitat, trail construction or maintenance, insect and disease control, or a combination of all of these activities. The area has been leased for oil and gas development.

A forest-improvement cut was conducted on the parcel in 2013.

UNIQUE FEATURES

- Example of sustainable northern hardwood management
- Unimproved logging road bisects property

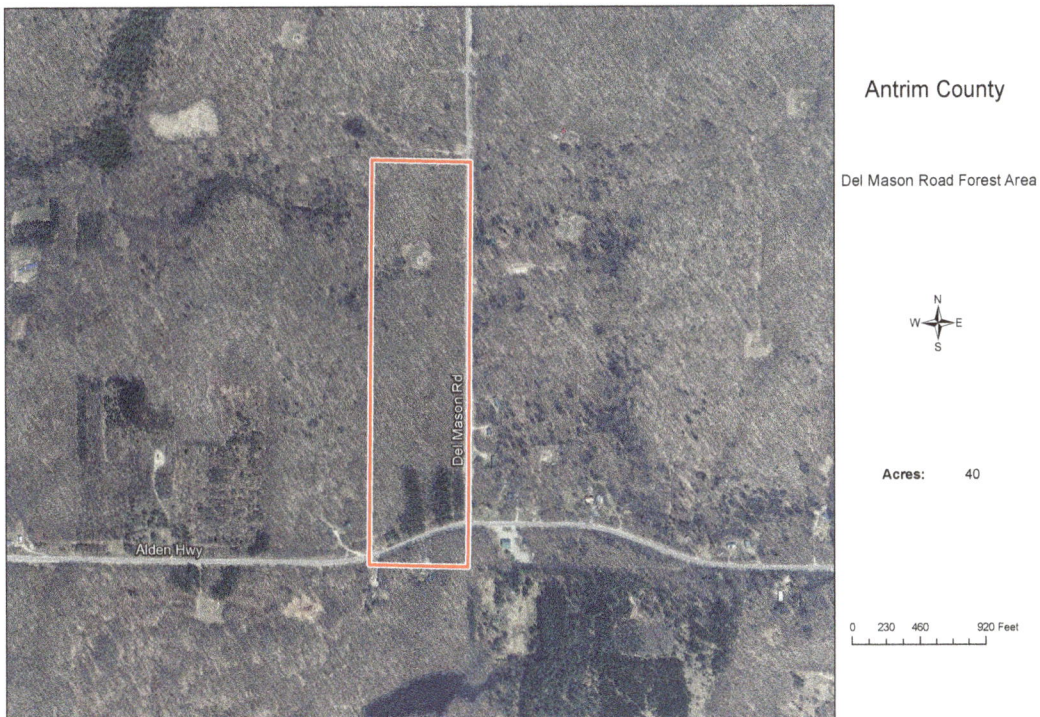

Antrim County

Del Mason Road Forest Area

Acres: 40

0 230 460 920 Feet

Notes:
The Del Mason Road Forest Area is accessed from Del Mason Rd.

Map Produced by
Antrim County Equalization
March 2023

53

Dickerson Road Forest Area

The Dickerson Road Forest Area is 250 acres of northern hardwood forest. It consists of rolling terrain with a few steep slopes. Logging roads exist on the parcel and are frequently used by hunters, hikers, snowmobiles, and other motorized vehicles.

This parcel has limited public ingress and egress. The property can be accessed through the Marcel Reiley Property, which is currently in the Commercial Forest Reserve Program administered by the State of Michigan. Informal access has been allowed from adjacent property owned by the Burns Family. The Vincent Family now owns the property. Historically, these families have not denied public access through their property.

The Dickerson Road Forest Area is an actively managed northern hardwood forest, where trees are periodically harvested for forest products, wildlife habitat, trail construction or maintenance, insect and disease control, or a combination of all these activities. This area has been leased for oil and gas development.

In 1973, the county conducted a large timber sale on the Echo Township Section 31 parcel. Pat Lacy was contracted to cut trees. The contract specified the cutting of all merchantable elm, beech, hemlock, and aspen. In addition, all maple, basswood, and ash sixteen inches in diameter and above were removed. This constituted the removal of 303,395 board feet of lumber products. Ron Meeder, of Meeder Lumber, purchased the wood products for $1,914.69.

In contrast, in 2022 the county sold 150 selected trees (33,318 board feet) for $52,655.

UNIQUE FEATURES

- Example of uneven-aged northern hardwood management
- Example of hemlock forest regeneration
- Extensive unimproved logging trails used for walking
- Scenic views

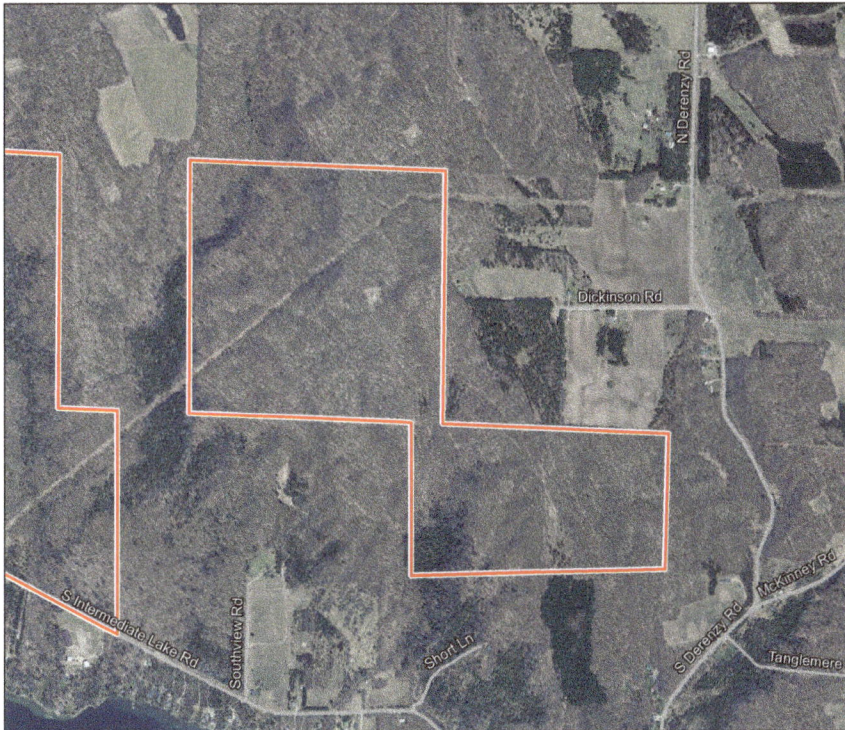

Antrim County

Dickerson Road Forest Area

Acres: 254

Notes:

The Dickerson Road Forest Area is accessed through private ownership with permission.

Map Produced by:
Antrim County Equalization
March 2023

55

Fred Prince Forest Area

The Fred Prince Estate donated the Fred Prince Forest Area to Antrim County in 2014.

No public access exists for this parcel at this time. The county purchased a forestry easement from the Warnes family in 2016, which allows for forest management and educational activities.

Ash killed by the invasive emerald ash borer and beech killed by beech bark disease were removed from the parcel in 2018.

Antrim County

Fred Prince Forest

N
W   E
S

Acres: 20

0   115   230   460 Feet

Notes:
The Fred Prince Forest has no public access. The County has a forestry easement from the Warens Family.

Map Produced by:
Antrim County Equalization
March 2023

Frog Hollow Forest Area

This parcel lies one quarter mile south of Shanty Creek Road. Frog Hollow Road is a dirt road that bisects this parcel. It contains forty acres of rolling northern hardwood forest with a strong red oak component. The parcel is easily accessed from Frog Hollow Road. The parcel is near the Shanty Creek / Schuss Mountain developments and is used extensively by hunters, hikers, cross-country skiers, and others.

The Frog Hollow Forest Area is an actively managed northern hardwood forest, where trees are periodically harvested for forest products, wildlife habitat, trail construction or maintenance, insect and disease control, or a combination of all these activities.

Several improvement cuts have aimed at increasing the oak component in the area.

UNIQUE FEATURES

- Example of northern hardwood management
- Unique oak component to this area

Antrim County

Frog Hollow Forest Area

Acres: 40

0   115   230   460 Feet

Notes:
The Frog Hollow Forest Area is accessed from Frog Hollow Road off of Shanty Creek Road.

Map Produced by:
Antrim County Equalization
March 2023

Glacial Hills Forest Area

The Glacial Hills Forest area is 288 acres and is contiguous with the larger (320 acre) Walter Kirkpatrick Forest Area. Combined they represent the largest community forest property owned by Antrim County. It consists of rolling terrain with a few steep slopes. Access to this area is from the Glacial Hills Pathway parking areas on Vandermark and Orchard Hill Roads, with other walk-in sites available. Logging roads exist on the parcel and are frequently used by hunters, hikers, snowmobiles, and other motorized vehicles.

The Glacial Hills Forest Area is an actively managed northern hardwood forest, where trees are harvested periodically for forest products, wildlife habitat, trail construction or maintenance, insect and disease control, or a combination of all of these.

Organized commercial harvesting activities began in 2016; this harvest focused on general thinning and the removal of dead and declining ash and beech trees.

The parcel is contiguous to the properties owned by Forest Home Township and the Village of Bellaire: collectively they are considered the Glacial Hills Pathway and Natural Area.

UNIQUE FEATURES
- Example of uneven-aged hardwood forest
- Example of ash removal
- Unimproved drive-through access
- Contains bike and hiking trails

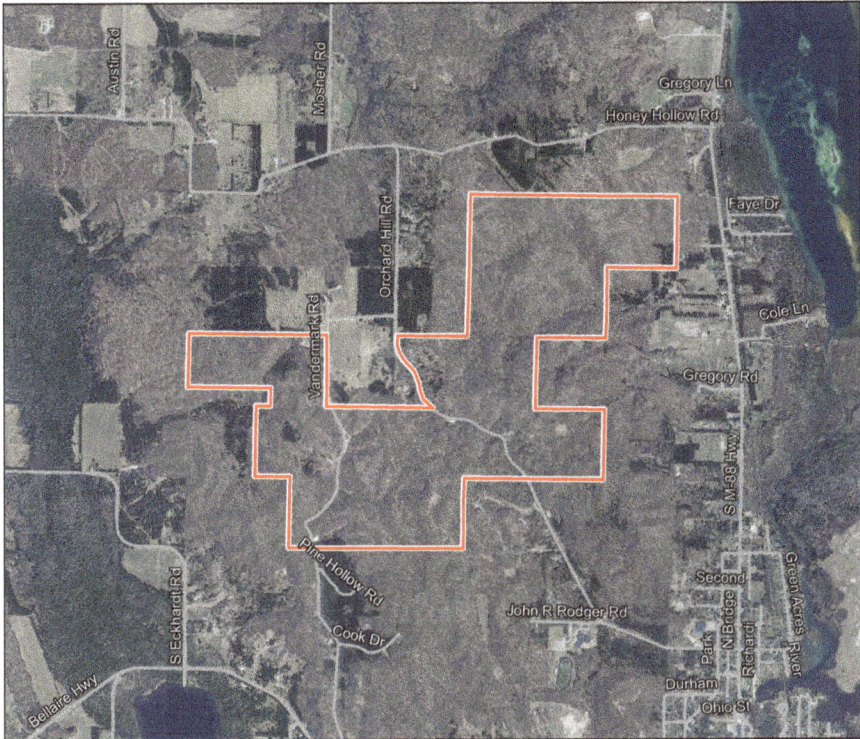

Antrim County

Glacial Hills Forest Area

Acres: 640

0   650   1,300   2,600 Feet

Notes:

Part of the Glacial Hills Natural Area. Jointly owned by Antrim County, Forest Home Township and Village of Bellaire. It contains the Glacial Hills Pathway, which is a mountain bike trail.

Map Produced by
Antrim County Equalization
March 2023

Hawk Lake Forest Area

The Hawk Lake Forest Area contains 160 acres and is contiguous with Mancelona Public School forest lands to the west. The area adjoins the Deward Management Area, which is part of the Mackinaw State Forest.

The area lies on the north side of Highway C-38 and is approximately seven miles east of Mancelona.

The area is primarily a red pine plantation. Aspen management and northern hardwood forest also exist on the parcel. The large-diameter pine plantation is in its fifth cutting rotation.

The parcel is accessed from Highway C-38, which bisects the southeast corner of the property. In addition, the parcel contains approximately 150 feet of lake shore on Hawk Lake, a small, relatively shallow inland lake on the south side of Highway C-38.

The area is used by bird hunters, deer hunters, and rabbit hunters in the fall and ORV users throughout the year. The lake is relatively unused due to low water levels and limited access.

The Hawk Lake Forest Area is an actively managed forest system, where trees are harvested for forest products, wildlife habitat, trail construction or maintenance, insect and disease control, or a combination of these activities.

The area has been leased for oil and gas development.

Hawk Lake was the first parcel the county acquired under the Municipal Forest Act.

UNIQUE FEATURES
- Red pine plantation management
- The establishment of white oak as part of the long-term forest management
- Unimproved access to Hawk Lake

HAWK LAKE FOREST—A SUCCESS STORY
The Hawk Lake Forest parcel represents the first parcel purchased by the county in 1936. The vacant property was quickly planted with trees. Fortunately, red pine was selected as the primary species to be planted; 108,000 red pine and 3,000 jack

Map Produced by
Antrim County Equalization
March 2023

Notes:

The Hawk Lake Forest Area can be accessed from Mancelona Road. It contains multiple use trails and adjoins state lands.

pine were planted in 1938. At the time, there were no foreseeable markets for red pine. Today red pine is highly marketable for treated lumber products, utility poles, and cabin logs.

Commercial harvesting on this parcel began in 1973. All the jack pine was removed from the plantation, 528 cords were harvested, and the county was paid $1,921.42 for the trees.

The Hawk Lake tree planting program would continue to produce revenue through periodic thinning projects.

- 1989 sold $15,769 of utility poles
- 1993 sold $14,356.80 pulpwood and pine bolt wood
- 1995 sold $16,725 pine products
- 2002 sold $6,600 cabin logs

- 2003 sold $55,000 pine products
- 2009 sold $5,000 cabin logs
- 2010 sold $22,000 pine products
- 2017 sold $78,000 pine and hardwood products
- **Total Value sold to date = $215,372.22**

The Hawk Lake Pine Plantation has reached its economic potential relative to timber value. Today, an estimated 4,680 cords of pine are still standing and available for harvest. The value of this resource is estimated at $327,600. Future management of this plantation will be aimed at removing mature red pine and re-establishing new trees through tree planting. The ACD forester decided to allow some of this acreage to be retained in larger diameter red pine.

Intermediate River Forest Area

The Intermediate River Forest Area is an forty-acre parcel. It is part of the Elk River Chain of Lakes Watershed headwaters. This parcel is primarily wetland complexes with riparian forest of cedar and hemlock. Beavers have created marshland habitats throughout this parcel. The old state road provides access to these acres. An unimproved access easement has been purchased from Leon Beal. The parcel is frequently used by hunters, fishermen, and the occasional brave hiker. It is maintained as watershed protection and wildlife.

UNIQUE FEATURES

- Wetland complexes including marshes created by historical beaver activity
- Deer yarding area
- Elk River Chain of Lakes Watershed headwaters area

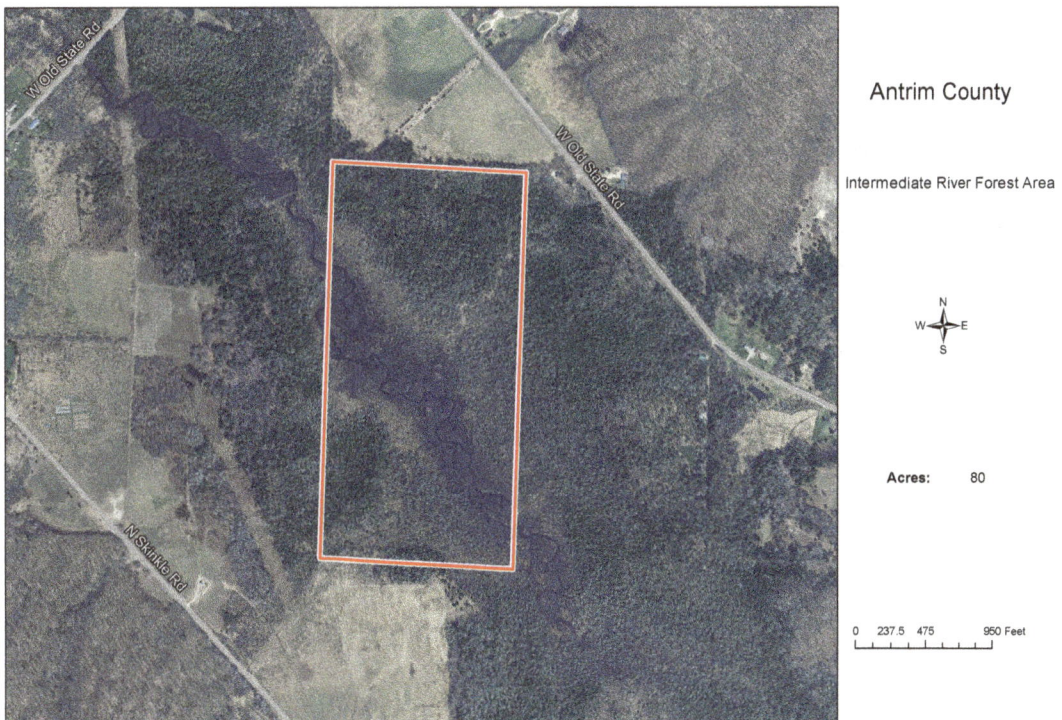

Antrim County

Intermediate River Forest Area

Acres: 80

0   237.5   475   950 Feet

Notes:
Part of the larger "Hitchcock Swamp". This parcel contains part of the headwaters of the Intermediate River (Chain of Lakes). There is an unimproved easement through Leon Beals property. Walk in only.

Map Produced by:
Antrim County Equalization
March 2023

Lake of the Woods Forest Area

The Lake of the Woods Forest Area is forty acres of northern hardwood forest with a strong oak component. It consists of rolling terrain. Access to this parcel is from Lake of the Woods Road. This parcel provides a primitive boat launch to Lake of the Woods. In addition, a small day park provides access to the lake for swimming and picnicking.

This parcel is an actively managed northern hardwood forest, where trees are periodically harvested for forest products, wildlife habitats, insect and disease control, or a combination of all these activities.

Planned commercial forest management activities began in 1996 and have been aimed at controlling oak wilt in the area.

UNIQUE FEATURES

- Day use access to Lake of the Woods
- Unique northern hardwood forest with an oak component impacted by oak wilt
- Small vernal pool

Antrim County

Lake of the Woods Forest Area

Acres: 40

0   130   260   520 Feet

Notes:
The Lake of the Woods Forest Area contains an unimproved - carry in boat launch and a small day park on the shore of Lake of the North. It is accessed from Lake of the Woods Road.

Map Produced by:
Antrim County Equalization
March 2023

Lake of the North 40 Forest Area

This is one of two parcels owned by Antrim County within the Lakes of the North development. This parcel is forty acres in size. It consists of natural white pine forest and aspen forest converting to northern hardwood forest. The parcel is flat in terrain.

Access to this acreage is from Wildwood Drive, which the county acquired to provide access for forest management purposes. Campers Village borders the north property line but does not provide public access to the property. Several ORV trails exist on the parcel and are frequently used by campers, hunters, hikers, snowmobiles, and other motorized vehicles.

The Lakes of the North 40 Forest Area is an actively managed forest, where trees are periodically harvested for forest products, wildlife habitat, trail construction or maintenance, insect and disease control, or a combination of all these activities.

In 2018 a forest stand improvement project was conducted on the property. This area has been leased for oil and gas development.

UNIQUE FEATURES

- Natural white pine forest under management
- Some remnant old-growth white pine still exists on property
- Unimproved trail system used for walking, hiking, and bird watching

Antrim County

Lake of the North Forest Area

Acres: 41

0   120   240   480 Feet

Notes:
The Lake of the North 40 can be accessed from Wildwood Drive. It contains some walking trails open to the public.

Map Produced by:
Antrim County Equalization
March 2023

Lake of the North 20 Forest Area

This is one of two parcels owned by Antrim County within the Lakes of the North development. This parcel is twenty acres in size. It primarily consists of aspen forest. The parcel is relatively flat in terrain.

Access to this area is from Valley Way Drive within the Lakes of the North development.

Aspen products were removed in 2013 for wildlife habitat improvement.

UNIQUE FEATURES

- Example of aspen management for wildlife purposes

Antrim County

Lake of the North 20

Acres: 20

0   140   280   560 Feet

Notes:

The Lake of the North 20 can be accessed from Valleyway Drive withing Lake of the North Association. There are no trails on this parcel.

Map Produced by:
[illegible]
March 2023

Leonard Road Forest Area

The Leonard Road Forest Area is eighty acres of northern hardwood forest. It consists of rolling terrain. Leonard Road bisects this property and provides walk-in access to this area. Logging roads exist on the parcel and are frequently used by hunters and hikers.

The Leonard Road Forest Area is an actively managed northern hardwood forest, where trees are harvested periodically for forest products, wildlife habitat, trail construction or maintenance, insect and disease control, or a combination of all these activities.

Organized commercial forest management activities began in 1994 and have since generated $190,322.26 in revenue through the sale of forest products.

UNIQUE FEATURES

- Example of uneven-aged northern hardwood forest management
- Example of black cherry and hemlock components to northern hardwood forest management
- Some unimproved walking opportunities

Antrim County

Leonard Road Forest Area

Acres: 80

0   190   380   780 Feet

Notes:
The Leonard Road Forest Area is accessed from Leonard Road. There are no formal trails. Open to public.

Map Produced by:
Antrim County Equalization
March 2023

Lewis Road Forest Area

The Lewis Road Forest Area is eighty acres of high-quality northern hardwood forest. It consists of rolling terrain with a few steep slopes. There is no public access to this parcel. The county does own a forestry easement for the purposes of forest management. Logging roads exist on the parcel and are frequently used by neighboring property owners for hunting, hiking, snowmobiles, and other motorized vehicles.

The Lewis Road Forest Area is an actively managed northern hardwood forest, where trees are periodically harvested for forest products, wildlife habitat, trail construction or maintenance, insect and disease control, or a combination of all these activities.

This area has been leased for oil and gas development.

Organized commercial forest management activities began in 1986 and have since generated $76,200.40 in revenue through the sale of forest products.

UNIQUE FEATURES

- Example of uneven-aged northern hardwood forest

Antrim County

Lewis Road Forest Area

Acres: 80

0   190   380   760 Feet

Notes:
The Lewis Road Forest Area has no public access at this time. The county has a forestry easement for management purposes through the Glen Derenzy property.

Map Produced by:
Antrim County Equalization
March 2023

Lore Road Forest Area

The Lore Road Forest Area is a forty-acre parcel located north of Eastport. It is currently landlocked with no public access. It contains lowland hardwood forest with a small northern hardwood forest component. It is considered mostly wetlands and is maintained for wildlife.

UNIQUE FEATURES

- Wetlands/lowland hardwood forest complex

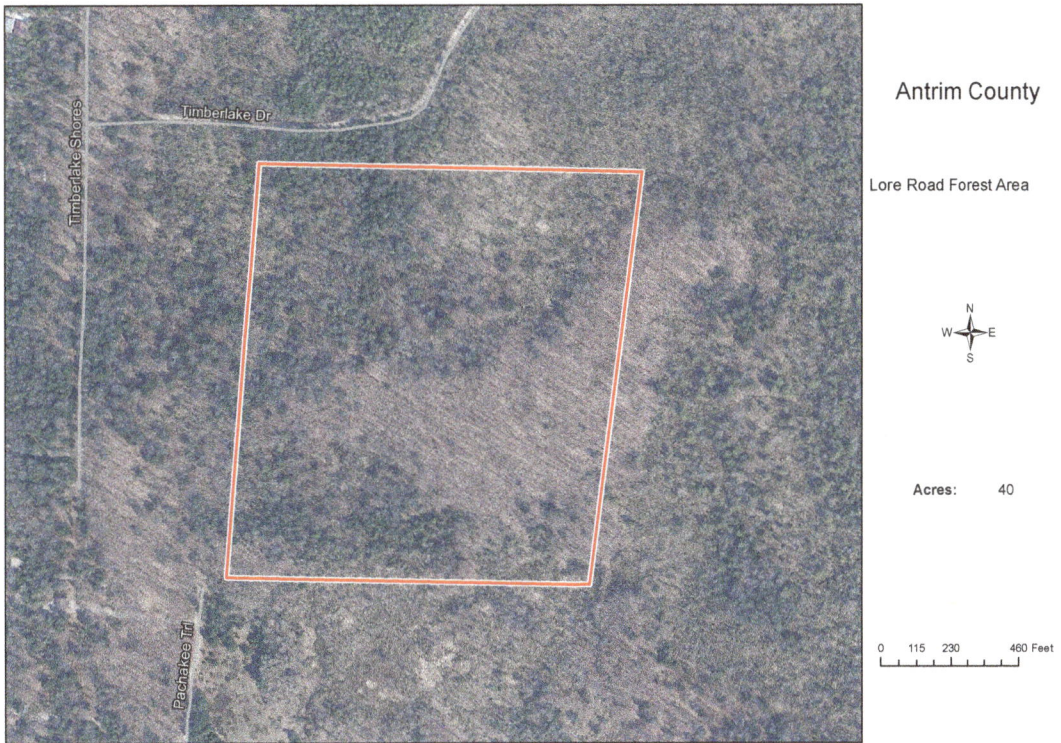

Antrim County

Lore Road Forest Area

Acres: 40

0   115   230   460 Feet

Notes:

The Lore Road 40 is currently landlocked and has no public access.

Map Produced by
Antrim County Equalization
March 2023

Mohrmann Park Natural Area & Forest Area

Mohrmann Park Natural Area & Forest Area contain 187.5 acres of forest land. The Mohrmann Park Natural Area was dedicated to the Mohrmann Family in 2017. The property, formerly known as Mohrmann Park, was dedicated to the four members of the Mohrmann family who served as Antrim County clerks during the period of 1922–2013. The Mohrmann Park Natural Area contains walking trails and a rustic picnic area.

The forest area contains rolling to steep terrain. The forest is actively managed northern hardwood forest, where trees have been harvested for forest products, wildlife habitat, insect and disease control, or a combination of all of these.

Fisk Creek bisects the property. The riparian corridor along both sides of Fisk Creek contains cedar or hemlock forests, which exhibit some old-growth characteristics.

Access is limited to walk-in only. Parking is available within the Natural Area off Intermediate Lake Road.

UNIQUE FEATURES

- Undisturbed stream corridors
- Old growth white cedar complexes
- Examples of uneven-aged northern hardwood forest
- Easily accessed and flat trail system

Antrim County

Mohrmann Forest Area

Acres: 187.5

0   425   850   1,700 Feet

Notes:
The Mohrmann Forest Area is accessed from Intermediate Lake Road at the Mohrmann Park.

Map Produced by:
Antrim County Equalization
March 2023

Morris Road Forest Area

The Morris Road Forest Area is 120 acres of northern hardwood forest. It consists of rolling terrain with a few steep slopes. Access is limited to walk-in access through state land to the west. Verbal access for the purposes of forest management activities has been granted by the Malpass Family in the past.

The Morris Road Forest Area is an actively managed northern hardwood forest, where trees are periodically harvested for forest products, wildlife habitat, maintenance, insect and disease control, or a combination of all these activities.

Planned commercial forest management activities began in 1981 and have since generated $90,000 in revenue.

UNIQUE FEATURES

- Example of uneven-aged northern hardwood forest management.

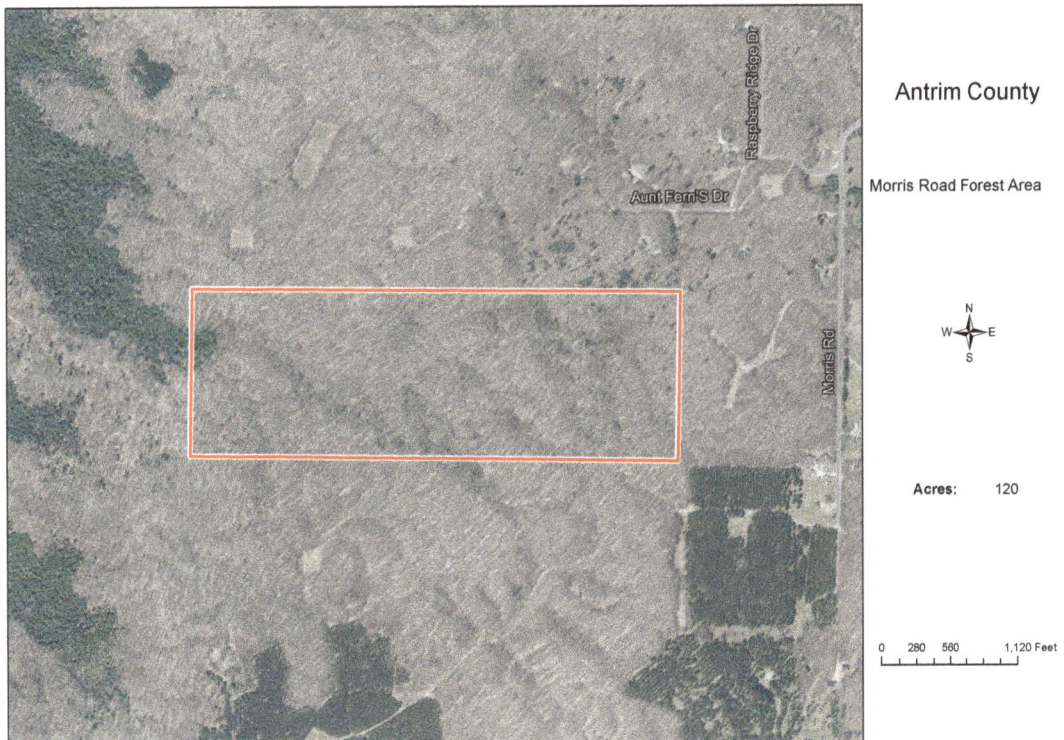

Antrim County

Morris Road Forest Area

Acres: 120

0   280   560   1,120 Feet

Notes:
The Morris Road Forest Area has no public access at this time.

Map Produced by:
Antrim County Equalization
March 2023

Murphy Park Forest Area

Murphy Park Forest Area is a seventy-three-acre forest area of northern hardwood forest and pine plantations. It consists of rolling terrain with a few steep slopes. Access to this acreage is from the Dunsmore Cemetery Road off County Road 624. Logging roads exist on the parcel and are frequently used by hunters and hikers.

Murphy Park Forest Area was named after the Murphy Family.

The Murphy Park Forest Area is an actively managed northern hardwood forest, where trees are periodically harvested for forest products, wildlife habitat, trail construction or maintenance, insect and disease control, or a combination of all these activities. This area has been leased for oil and gas development.

Planned commercial forest management activities began in 1986 and have since generated $50,640.40 in revenue through the sale of forest products. Pine plantations are in their fourth cutting rotation.

UNIQUE FEATURES

- Managed red and white pine plantations
- Example of northern hardwood forest management

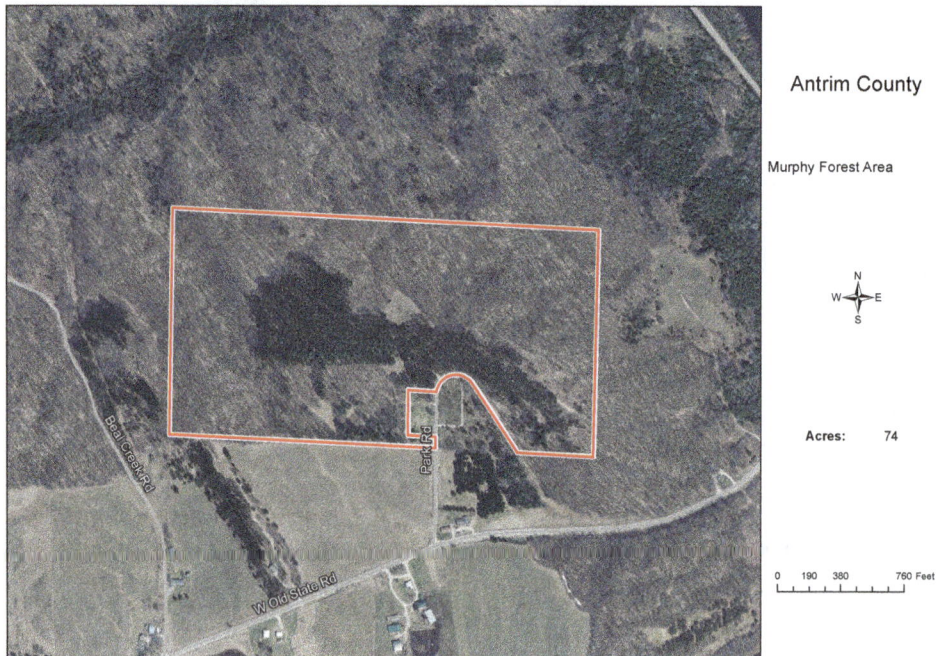

Antrim County

Murphy Forest Area

Acres: 74

0   190   380   760 Feet

Notes:

Map Produced by:
Antrim County Equalization
March 2023

Pete Wilks Forest Area

The Pete Wilks Forest Area is 98.40 acres of northern hardwood forest including a pine forest and aspen. This forest area was dedicated to Mr. Pete Wilks, who served as Antrim County commissioner in the early 1990s. Pete served on the Antrim County Parks and Lands Committee, which was dedicated to protecting and utilizing our county forest areas.

The property consists of rolling terrain with a few steep slopes. Access to this area is from the gravel pit on Derenzy Road and from Ritt Road, which borders the north side of the property. Logging roads exist on the parcel and are frequently used by hunters and hikers. The parcel is restricted to walk-in access only.

The Pete Wilks Forest Area is a high-quality, actively managed northern hardwood forest, where trees are periodically harvested for forest products, wildlife habitat, road maintenance, insect and disease control, or a combination of all these activities.

Planned commercial forest management activities began in 1994 and have since generated $136,071.36 in revenue through the sale of forest products.

UNIQUE FEATURES

- Example of uneven-aged northern hardwood forest management
- Unimproved logging roads used for walking and bird-watching
- Scenic views

Antrim County

Pete Wilks Forest Area

Acres: 98.4

0 190 380 760 Feet

Notes:
The Pete Wilks Forest Area is a managed hardwood forest area. Can be accessed from Ritt Road or Derenzy Road.

Map Produced by
Antrim County Equalization
March 2023

73

Simpson Road Forest Area

The Simpson Road Forest Area is 160 acres of northern hardwood forest, pine plantations, and a wetland. It consists of rolling terrain with a few steep slopes. Access to this acreage is from Simpson Road, which borders the north side of the property. Logging roads exist on the parcel and are frequently used by hunters, hikers, snowmobiles, and other motorized vehicles.

The Simpson Road Forest Area is an actively managed northern hardwood forest, where trees are periodically harvested for forest products, wildlife habitat, trail construction or maintenance, insect and disease control, or a combination of all these activities.

This area has been leased for oil and gas development.

Planned commercial forest management activities began in 1986 and have since generated $90,640.40 in revenue through the sale of forest products.

UNIQUE FEATURES

- Example of uneven-aged northern hardwood forest
- Example of red and white pine plantation management
- Small marshland/wetland complex
- Unimproved logging roads provide drive-through access to most of the property

Antrim County

Simpson Road Forest Area

W Simpson Rd

Getaway Ln

S M-88 Hwy

Acres: 160

0   235   470   940 Feet

Notes:

The Simpson Road Forest Area can be accessed from Simpson Road. It contains some multiple use trails.

Map Produced by
Antrim County Equalization
March 2023

Skinkle Road Forest Area

The Skinkle Road Forest Area is 160 diverse acres of northern hardwood forest, a red pine plantation, and wetlands. It consists of rolling to steep terrain and can be difficult to navigate for new visitors. The property is easily accessed from Skinkle Road. Several logging roads provide interior, which is open to foot traffic and vehicles.

The Skinkle Road Forest Area is an actively managed forest, where trees are harvested for forest products and wildlife habitat.

It is located near hundreds of acres of state lands, part of the Mackinaw State Forest, and is available for public usage.

This area has been leased for oil and gas development.

UNIQUE FEATURES

- Example of uneven-aged northern hardwood forest management
- Stream and wetland complexes
- Some drive-in access available

Antrim County

Skinkle Road Forest Area

Acres: 150

0   230   460   920 Feet

Notes:
The Skinkle Road Forest Area is accessed from Skinkle Road.

Map Produced by:
Antrim County Equalization
March 2023

Star Township 40 Forest Area

The Star Township 40 Forest Area contains 40 acres of an actively managed northern hardwood forest and a red pine plantation where trees are periodically harvested for forest products, wildlife habitat, trail construction or maintenance, insect and disease control, or a combination of all of these activities.

This area has been leased for oil and gas development.

A hardwood stand improvement project was completed in 2005. This project generated $15,000 in revenue and set up this forest for future revenue.

The Star Township 40 Forest Area is somewhat difficult to find. The county does have a public access easement through the Lamberson Property. From Alba travel east two miles on C-42 Road. Go north on Tobias Road 2.5 miles to Sand Hill Road. Travel east on Sand Hill Road 1.5 miles. Travel north on a small two-track 0.25 miles to the southern property line.

UNIQUE FEATURES

- Example of uneven-aged northern hardwood forest management
- Red pine plantation and example of successful tree planting

Antrim County

Star 40

Acres: 40

0   115   230   460 Feet

Notes:
These acres are accessed through a purchased easement from the Lamberson Family.

Map Produced by:
Antrim County Equalization
March 2023

Valley Road Forest Area

The Valley Road Forest Area is a forty-one acre parcel located west of Mancelona. It can be accessed from Valley Road and has walk-in access only. It contains high-quality northern hardwood forest, a red pine plantation, and a small six-acre area where Scotch pine was removed in 1994. It consists of rolling terrain. Logging roads exist on the parcel and are frequently used by hunters and hikers.

The Valley Road Forest Area is an actively managed northern hardwood forest, where trees are periodically harvested for forest products, wildlife habitat, trail construction or maintenance, insect and disease control, or a combination of all these activities. This property was one of the first forests impacted by beech bark disease in Antrim County.

Forest improvement cuts have been conducted in the pine and hardwood forests beginning in 1994. The property has generated $16,000 in revenue through periodic thinning practices.

UNIQUE FEATURES

- Example of red pine plantation management in its second rotation
- Example of northern hardwood forest management

Antrim County

Valley Road Forest Area

N
W — E
S

Acres: 40

0   137.5 275   550 Feet

Notes:

The Valley Road parcel can be accessed from Valley Road.

Map Produced by:
Antrim County Equalization
March 2023

79

Walter Kirkpatrick Forest Area

In 2011, 320 acres in Forest Home Township were dedicated to Mr. Kirkpatrick as a memorial forest area. Today, these 320 acres are part of the Glacial Hills Pathway and continue to provide recreational opportunities, forestry education, and forest revenue for the county.

The Walter Kirkpatrick Forest Area is located to the east of the Glacial Hills Pathway and Natural Area. The Walter Kirkpatrick Forest Area was dedicated to Mr. Kirkpatrick for his lifelong love and dedication to the forests here in Antrim County. Mr. Kirkpatrick, along with Raymond Murphy and Edgar Wright, were responsible for the acquisition of much of the county-owned forest lands in the 1940s and '50s.

Antrim County received this property in conjunction with several parcels from the State of Michigan's Municipal Forest Act. The land was deeded to the county to be utilized for forestry purposes. The term, "forestry purposes," relates to the management of this parcel for the production of forest products, as well as forestry education within the community.

The county agreed to utilize the Walter Kirkpatrick Forest Area in conjunction with the Glacial Hills Pathway and Natural Area & Forest Area for the possible expansion of recreations trails to access the Village of Bellaire and other public properties.

This property contains an enormous opportunity for the county to provide recreation opportunities for local residents, to attract visitors, to educate the public regarding sustainable forestry, to generate income through the sale of forest products and natural gas, and to protect open space and wildlife habitats.

UNIQUE FEATURES

- Example of northern hardwood management
- Scenic views

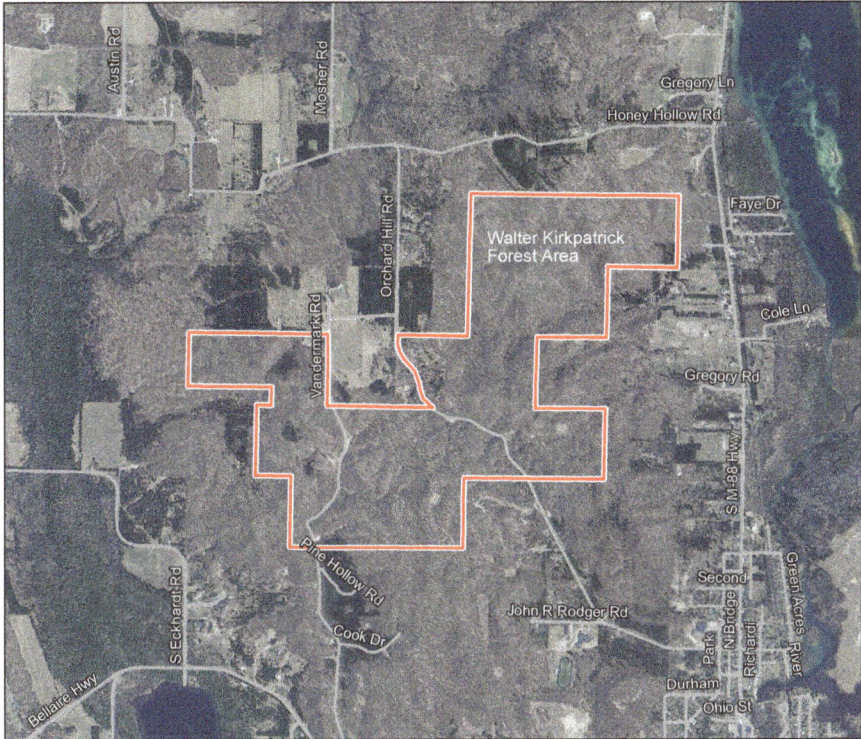

Antrim County

Glacial Hills Forest Area

Walter Kirkpatrick
Forest Area

Acres: 640

0   650   1,300   2,600 Feet

Map Produced by
Antrim County Equalization
March 2023

Notes:

Part of the Glacial Hills Natural Area. Jointly owned by Antrim County, Forest Home Township and Village of Bellaire. It contains the Glacial Hills Pathway, which is a mountain bike trail.

NATURAL AREA LANDS

The Antrim County Board of Commissioners has designated or has recognized some county ownerships as "natural areas." Often these natural area designations overlap those designated as community forest areas. It is recognized that forest lands exist on most of those properties designated as natural areas. Each natural area is managed in partnership with different groups, who have worked with the county forester and developed management plans.

Natural Area	Acreage	Management Partner
Antrim Creek Natural Area	156	Friends of Antrim Creek, GTRLC
Cedar River Natural Area	226	Friends of Cedar River, Village of Bellaire, GTRLC
Glacial Hills Pathway and Natural Area	763	Friends of Glacial Hills, GTRLC
Grass River Natural Area	1,492	Grass River Natural Area, Inc.
Mohrmann Park Natural Area	12	Parks Director
TOTAL	2,649	

Table 6: Designated Natural Areas

Antrim Creek Natural Area

Location: 9890 Old Dixie Highway & Rex Beach Road, Ellsworth

Natural Features:
- One mile of Lake Michigan shoreline
- Cobblestone beach
- Sand dunes
- A portion of Antrim Creek

Natural Communities:
- Northern hardwood forest
- Meadow
- Coastal dune
- Forested wetland
- Conifer swamp
- Shrub thicket
- Wet meadow

Recreational Opportunities:
- Trails
- Parking areas (3)
- Restrooms
- Beach access

Acquisition: 1996, acquired by Antrim County

Management: Managed by Antrim County Commissioners

This natural area was established in 1996 (see above on page 19). It supports a wide range of flora and fauna including federal- and state-listed threatened plant species. This is a rare and unique coastal ecosystem without equal. Many residents

and visitors enjoy pursuing leisure time recreational activities in the beautiful natural habitats of Antrim Creek.

The Antrim Creek Natural Area offers a unique experience due to the presence of rare natural features, including diverse wildlife habitats and federally protected plant species.

For location trail and parking maps see GTRLC.org website.

Cedar River Natural Area & Forest Area

Location: Stover Road, east of Bellaire

Natural Features:
- 6,395 feet of frontage on Cedar River
- Michigan Blue Ribbon Trout Stream
- Undisturbed stream corridor

Natural Communities:
- Remnant old growth white cedar and white pine
- Hemlock forest
- Lowland conifer swamp
- Red pine plantation

Recreational Opportunities:
- Interpretive signage
- Reconstucted historical train bridge
- River access for fishing
- Two miles of hiking trails
- Connection to Craven Park Campgrounds and Antrim County Fairgrounds
- Open to hunting, fishing, and trapping during the designated seasons as regulated by the Michigan Department of Natural Resources

Acquisition: 2000

The Cedar River Natural Area contains 233+/- acres of property jointly owned by Antrim County and the Village of Bellaire. Within the natural area are 6,395 feet of stream frontage and two miles of hiking trails. The natural area is open year-round to visitors and residents alike. It is open to hunting, fishing, and trapping during the designated seasons as regulated by the Michigan Department of Natural Resources. It adjoins the Antrim County Fairgrounds and the Craven Park Campground run by the Village of Bellaire.

The Cedar River Natural Area was established in 2000 with the purchase of the seventy-eight acres known as the Skaff Property. The county's goal was to protect the pristine wetlands, river frontage, and unique wildlife habitats. The Skaff Property adjoins the Village of Bellaire properties where forty-six acres have been dedicated to the natural area.

Notes:

The Cedar River Natural Area includes property owned by the Village of Bellaire and Antrim County. It contains 2 miles of walking trails, river frontage and a variety of forest types. Open to public.

Map Produced by:
Antrim County Equalization
March 2023

The county was able to expand the natural area by purchasing 109 acres from the Jabara Family in 2002. This allowed the county to expand the existing trail system owned by the Village of Bellaire. This trail includes the railroad grade and adjoining trails that traverse the property. Trails can be wet at times, so boots may be required for some trail usage.

Access to the natural area is from three trailheads: at the Antrim County Fairgrounds, off Stover Road, and off Burrell Road. Walk-in access only.

The Cedar River Forest Area is actively managed for recreation, stream, and wetland protection, and wildlife habitat. Some harvesting has occurred to improve wildlife, construct or maintain trails, control insects or diseases, or a combination of all these activities.

Glacial Hills Pathway and Natural Area & Forest Area

Location: West and north of Bellaire

Natural Communities:
- Northern hardwood forest
- Dry-mesic hardwood forest
- Shrub thicket
- Wet mesic forest

Recreational Opportunities:
- Three trailheads (Eckhardt Road, Vandermark Road, Orchard Hill)
- 31.5 miles of trails for mountain biking, hiking, hunting, wildlife viewing, winter sports
- Trail signage
- Parking areas

Acquisition:

It was moved by Blackmore, seconded by Allen that Mike Meriwether enter into negotiations with Mark Sevald for purchase of approximately 50 acres of commercial forest reserve land in Section 14 of Forest Home township at a price not to exceed $2,000 per acre with conditions that Antrim County retain outright ownership of the property, the funds for the purchase be paid from the Forestry Fund, and Forest Home Township use the county's purchase amount as a cash match for the potential Michigan Natural Resources Trust Fund grant application for the acquisition of adjoining properties. Motion carried by a yea and nay vote as follows: Yes — McLeod, Dawson, Bargy, White, Howelman, Crawford, Stanek, Blackmore, Allen; No — None; Absent — None.

The Antrim County-owned portion of the Glacial Hills Natural Area consists of 288 acres. The area consists of the consolidation of 118 acres of historically owned county forest land with the 170 acres of the Sevald Property (2011).

The Sevald property was the keystone to forming a contiguous area for a trail system that would be located entirely on public land. The strategic location of the Sevald property made it especially attractive for the establishment of a recreational area in conjunction with the Forest Home Township efforts. In 2011, Forest Home Township was able to acquire much of the remaining Sevald Estate (175 acres). These acres are contiguous and to the west of the county-owned acreages. This area is known as the Glacial Hills Pathway and Natural Area. It is owned jointly by the township and Antrim County.

The natural area was created with a joint effort and financial contributions by the Olsen Family Trust, Grand Traverse Regional Land Conservancy, Forest Home Township, private citizens, the Michigan Trust Fund, and Antrim County.

Both Forest Home Township and Antrim County have documented a desire to establish a trail system linking the Village of Bellaire with public lands in Forest Home Township.

Antrim County worked with Forest Home Township and the Village of Bellaire in developing the Glacial Hills Pathway. The Village of Bellaire added forty acres from what was formerly the Village Dump site. The Glacial Hills Pathway project is an effort to establish a trail system throughout the joint ownerships and linked to existing public recreational areas.

Over time, connections will be made to link downtown Bellaire, the popular Bellaire Bike Trail, the Bellaire Public Schools and Athletic Complex, the Rotary Soccer Field, Richardi Park on the Intermediate River, as well as the Bellaire

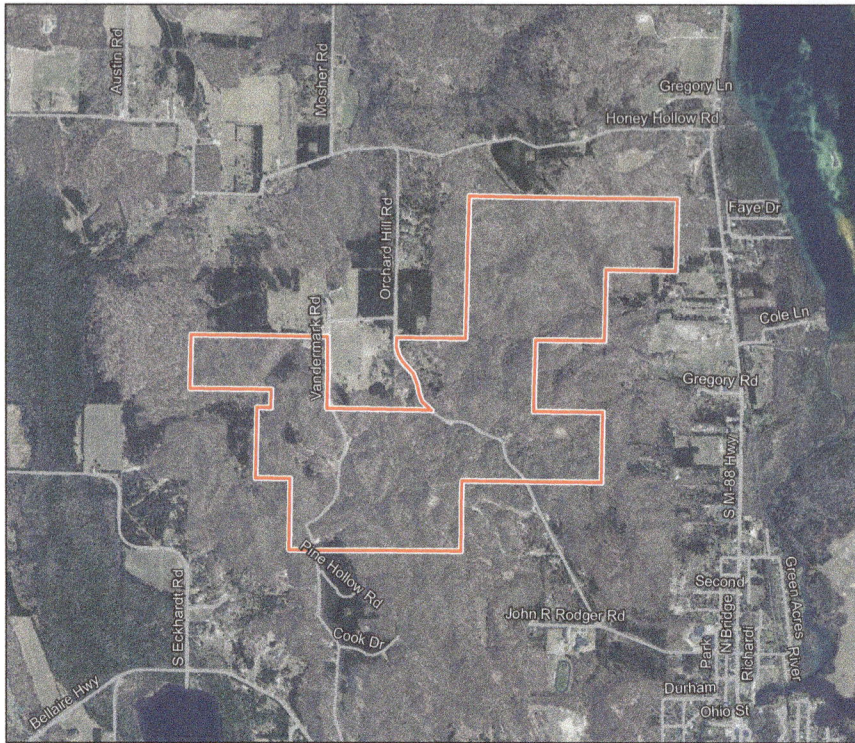

Antrim County

Glacial Hills Forest Area

Acres: 640

0   650 1,300   2,600 Feet

Notes:
Part of the Glacial Hills Natural Area. Jointly owned by Antrim County, Forest Home Township and Village of Bellaire. It contains the Glacial Hills Pathway, which is a mountain bike trail.

Map Produced by:
Antrim County Equalization
March 2023

Baseball Fields. Other connections might include access to the Cedar River Natural Area, as well as the Grass River Natural Area.

In April of 2012, the Antrim County Commissioners approved the construction of a mountain bike trail on the Glacial Hills Pathway west of Vandermark Road.

ADMINISTRATION

The Glacial Hills Pathway and Natural Area & Forest Area is classified as county forest land. The Antrim County Board of Commissioners provides administrative oversight to the area. The Antrim Conservation District Forester manages the area. Through an intergovernmental agreement between the county, Forest Home Township, and the Village of Bellaire, the Friends of Glacial Hills Recreational Board was established for management and maintenance of the mountain biking and walking trails.

LEGAL DESCRIPTION AND DEED RESTRICTIONS

The Glacial Hills Natural Area contains four parcels acquired under Michigan's Municipal Forest Act (PA 451), as well as five parcels acquired through a grant agreement with the Michigan Trust Fund. The approved allocation from the Michigan Trust Fund required that the property be utilized for public recreation in perpetuity. PA 451 required that the property be utilized for forestry purposes.

Table 7 specifically describes individual parcels recorded with the Antrim County Equalization Department.

Parcel Description	Section and Township	Acres	Deed Restrictions
N ½, NE ¼	23 Forest Home	80	MTF
N ½, SE ¼, SW ¼	14 Forest Home	20	MTF
SW ¼, SW ¼, SE ¼ & SE ¼, SE ¼, SW ¼	14 Forest Home	20	MTF
N ½, SW ¼, SE ¼ & SE ¼, SW ¼, SW ¼	14 Forest Home	30	MTF
W ½, SE ¼, SE ¼	14 Forest Home	20	MTF
E ½, SE ¼, SE ¼	14 Forest Home	20	Municipal Forest
E ½, NE ¼, NW ¼	23 Forest Home	20	Municipal Forest
SW ¼, SE ¼, SW ¼	14 Forest Home	10	Municipal Forest
N ½, SW ¼, with Exc	14 Forest Home	68	Municipal Forest
Kirkpatrick Forest Area	14 Forest Home	320	Municipal Forest
MTF = Michigan Trust Fund			

Table 7: Glacial Hills Pathway and Natural Area Descriptions and Deed Restrictions

Grass River Natural Area

Location: 6500 Alden Highway, Bellaire

Natural Features: Grass River flows 2.5 miles from Lake Bellaire into Clam Lake

Natural Communities:
- Northern fen
- Northern wet meadow
- Rich conifer swamp
- Emergent marsh
- Northern shrub thicket
- Mesic hardwood forest
- Dry-mesic hardwood forest

Recreational Opportunities:
- 7.5 miles of trails, including boardwalks
- Nature center
- Dock & kayak launch on Grass River

Acquisition: 1979

Management: Grass River Natural Area, Inc. manages the natural area for Antrim County

Grass River Natural Area is a 1,492-acre nature preserve surrounding the Grass River, located in the heart of Antrim County. Along with the beautiful views of Grass River, we also offer seven miles of well-maintained trails including 1.5 miles of boardwalk floating above northern fen and cedar wetlands. With all these natural features, Grass River Natural Area offers visitors an outdoor, living laboratory to explore and learn. The Grass River Center is open year-round, offering a comfortable learning environment for public programming, school field trips, camps, and more.

In 1969 Grass River Natural Area was founded by a group of citizens concerned about the development of sensitive wetland habitat. Grass River Natural Area, Inc. is a 501(c)(3) nonprofit organization incorporated in 1979. We are under contract with Antrim County to manage the Grass River Natural Area for land protection, stewardship, conservation, and environmental education. The partnership between GRNA, Inc. and Antrim County was established in 1979 and is an important component of Grass River Natural Area's unique conservation story.

GRNA - Areas Open/Closed to Hunting

Its goals are to manage the Grass River Natural Area, conserve and protect its watershed, and provide opportunities that increase knowledge, appreciation, and community-wide stewardship of the natural environment.

Antrim County owns most of the 1,492 acres that make up Grass River Natural Area, and they also own the Grass River Center—our education building finished in 2011. The funds raised for the center were a result of a successful Capital Campaign coordinated and managed by Grass River Natural Area, Inc. in partnership with Antrim County.

Forestry in Grass River

Grass River has taken some steps to manage and maintain some of the forest eco-systems found on the property. In 2008, several small clear-cuts were conducted to manage and maintain the aspen component within the natural area. In 2014, a forest stand improvement project was conducted to demonstrate forestry practices within the natural area.

Forest Stand Improvement Project

The Grass River Natural Areas (GRNA) Conservation Committee has recommended that a minimum of ten acres of the natural area be devoted to forestry education. Although GRNA is 90% forested, much of these forest communities are wetland forests or riparian forests where forest management activities are limited by soil types, low species values, accessibility, and administrative policies.

The Natural Area contains 281 acres of identified upland hardwood forest. These forest acres are dominated by red maple, aspen, black cherry, and other associated species such as white pine, hemlock, and birch.

The upland forest within the GRNA is considered a second-growth forest. In other words, the forest has regrown from intensive cutting done in the past. Second-growth forests generally contain a high density of trees impacting growth. Trees originating from stump sprouting, trees of low quality, and off-site species are also common to these forest communities.

In the winter of 2014, trees within a designated management area were marked and cut to the ground by the county forester and other volunteers as part of a forest improvement project. The cutting was aimed at creating an educational area for visitors to the GRNA. Education is to focus on forest ecology, tree identification,

tree growth and development, wildlife, forest products, and other natural resource topics.

Here in GRNA, forest stand improvement cutting has been done to:

- Improve the quality and quantity of wood production
- Improve growing space for residual trees
- Initiate natural regeneration of trees in the forest
- Improve wildlife habitats
- Improve species diversity
- Restore and protect plant communities
- Provide educational opportunities

See grassriver.org for trail maps, location, interpretive center information, and other information regarding the Grass River Natural Area.

PARK LANDS

Antrim County owns and operates public campgrounds and several day-use areas. These properties are managed and maintained through the parks department.

Parks	Township	Acreage
Barnes Park	Banks	65
Beals Lake Boat Launch	Central Lake	1.39
Elk Rapids Day Park	Elk Rapids	12.31
Lake of the Woods Day Park	Kearney	1
Noteware's Landing	Kearney	1
Wetzel Lake Day Park	Mancelona	1
Willow Day Park	Custer	1

Table 8: Antrim County Park Lands

Barnes Park & Forest Area

Location: 12298 Barnes Park Road, Eastport, MI

Natural Features:
- Lake Michigan beach
- Sand dunes

Natural Communities:
- Unique oak forest complex
- Natural white pine complexes
- Unique wetlands
- Managed red pine plantations

Recreational Opportunities:
- 2.5 miles of trails (chipped and paved), including a Forest Interpretive Trail,
- used in for winter sports
- Beach access
- Campground with seventy campsites
- Pavilion
- Restrooms
- Ballfield and playground
- Parking area

Acquisition:

In 1939, Antrim County established the first county park on the shores of Lake Michigan in Eastport.

The Barnes Park Forest Area consists of privately-owned, smaller parcels pieced together from smaller parcels held under private ownership. Originally, the current park land and other acreages were given to the State of Michigan by the federal government for the purposes of aiding in the construction of a railroad from Grand Rapids to some point on Little Grand Traverse Bay. (An Act of Congress, June 3,

1856.) The State of Michigan conveyed larger acreages to the Grand Rapids and Indian Railroad. From this ownership, the private ownership and subsequent subdivision of Section One began. Over the years, the property was held in various descriptions by the State of Michigan, railroad companies, lumber companies, private owners, and non-profit groups such as the Eastport Racetrack Association and the Bay View Arbor of Gleaners Number 551.

In March of 1939, the Bay View Arbor Gleaners sold sixty-five acres to Antrim County for $1000.00. It was understood that the property conveyed to the county shall be open to the public at all times, in perpetuity.

In February of 1950, the State of Michigan conveyed an additional eighty acres to Antrim County. It was understood that these lands would be used solely for forestry purposes and would revert to the State if not managed for such purposes. The state also retained all rights to the minerals on the property, as well as public ingress and egress for the people of the State of Michigan. In addition, the state retained all aboriginal antiquities found on the parcel (See Historical Map 1, Parcel 2).

The remaining 42 +/- forested acres were conveyed to the county with no real restrictions. It was understood that the property would forever be open to the public. These undeveloped acres are valued and examined for their open space attributes, wildlife habitats, recreational potential, forest management potential, and the like.

The acquisition of the remaining 17.77 acres is unclear. These acres appear to be the southern part of Government Lot 3. The Cameron Lumber Company was the last owner of record, which was recorded in 1903. (See Historical Map 1, Parcel 3)

Currently, 156.74 acres make up Barnes Park and surrounding forest lands. A survey of these acres was conducted in March of 1999. (See Attachment Survey Map)

Beals Lake Boat Launch

Location: Six Mile Lake Road. 0.3 miles from the intersection of Old State Road (634) and Six Mile Lake Road. Pleasant Valley

Natural Features:
- Small inland lake

Natural Communities:
- Wetlands

Recreational Opportunities:
- Primitive boat launch

Acquisition: 1988

This primitive boat launch was purchased from the Beal Family for $5,050 in 1988. It was intended to provide fishing access to Beals Lake.

Management: Antrim County Parks Department

The Beals Lake Boat Launch is a public boat launch area providing access to Beals Lake. It is a carry-in access site primarily used in the winter for ice fishing.

Elk Rapids Day Park

The Elk Rapids Day Park is a unique park on the east shore of the Grand Traverse Bay. It is located within the village of Elk Rapids. There is a short walking trail with local artwork on display. The park has access to Lake Michigan for day-use activities.

Location: S. Bayshore Drive, Elk Rapids

Natural Features:
- Lake Michigan lake shore

Natural Communities:
- Oak forest

Recreational Opportunities:
- Outdoor sculpture park
- Trails
- Bath house pavilion
- Beach access
- Parking area

Acquisition: 1969

The Elk Rapids Day Park was acquired from the State of Michigan under Act 223 for recreational purposes. It contains a recreation reversion clause stating should the recreational usage no longer be utilized it shall revert back to the State of Michigan.

Management: Parks Department

Lake of the Woods Day Park

The county owns a small day park on the south shore of Lake of the North. It is contiguous with county forest lands. It offers swimming, shoreline fishing, and an unimproved boat launch.

Location: Park Trail, Bellaire

Natural Features:
- Adjoins county community forests
- Lake frontage on Lake of the Woods

Natural Communities:
- Northern hardwood forest with oak component

Recreational Opportunities:
- Swimming and day use
- Shore fishing
- Primitive boat launch

Acquisition: 2022
This small day park was given to the county in 2022 by Custer Township. The day park is maintained by the Parks Department.

Notewares Landing

Notewares Landing is a county-owned day park on the east shore of Lake Bellaire. It is used for swimming, shore fishing, and picnicking. There are public restrooms on-site and parking is available.

Location: Fisherman's Paradise Road, Bellaire

Natural Features:
- Lake Bellaire frontage

Recreational Opportunities:
- Swimming and day use
- Shore fishing
- Primitive boat launch

Acquisition: 1986

Acquired from the State of Michigan for public use under Act 233. A recreational reversion clause requires the property be utilized for public recreation.

Wetzel Lake Day Park

Wetzel Lake is a small day park on Wetzel Lake north and east of Mancelona. This is a unique collaboration between the Michigan Department of Natural Resources, the Village of Mancelona, the Antrim Conservation District, and Antrim County. This property has been leased from the MDNR for day park usage. It is primarily used for picnicking, swimming, and fishing. There is a public restroom, boat launch, and picnic tables available to visitors.

Location: Wetzel Lake Road, Mancelona Township

Natural Features:
- Adjoins 3,372 acres of state forest
- Lake frontage on Wetzel Lake

Natural Communities:
- Riparian shoreline

Recreational Opportunities:
- Swimming
- Picnic area
- Boat launch
- Shore fishing

Acquisition: Wetzel Lake is leased by Antrim County from the State of Michigan

Willow Day Park

Willow Day Park is contiguous to the Grass River Natural Area and is located on the east shoreline of Lake Bellaire. The county maintains this park as a day park area. It contains a public restroom and picnic area. Both carry-in boat launch and shore fishing are available.

Location: White Birch Lane, Bellaire

Natural Features:
- Lake Bellaire shoreline
- Connected to Grass River Natural Area

Natural Communities:
- Riparian to Lake Bellaire

Recreational Opportunities:
- **Lake Bellaire walk-in access**
- Picnic tables and grills
- Portable toilet

Acquisition: 2008

This small day park was acquired in conjunction with a larger land purchase organized by Grass River Inc. Natural Resource trust fund dollars were utilized as matching funds. Grass River Inc. sold the day park acre to the county for $56,250.

Management: Parks Department

MANAGING THREATS TO OUR FORESTS

Forest management planning is only a template or guideline for potential outcomes and activities occurring on a parcel. These plans need to be adaptable to the changing forest dynamics occurring. They also need to be able to adapt to changing property usages, market trends, and most recently threats/damaging agents such as insect and disease issues that have impacted forest planning.

First, we lost the elm trees to Dutch elm disease. Today, beech bark disease is impacting the forest. By now, most people are familiar with the emerald ash borer that decimated ash trees throughout the Great Lakes Basin. Forest tent caterpillars, gypsy moth outbreaks, and drought have all influenced county forest lands. It is important to spend a few minutes discussing these impacts on county forests.

Dutch Elm Disease (DED)

The American elm was once widely distributed throughout the Eastern United States. It was a preferred tree for use along city streets and yards of many homeowners. The DED fungal pathogen was introduced into the US in 1930, and was first identified in Cleveland, Ohio.

The disease likely came to this country on packing or shipping materials. By 1985, most of the elm trees within the US had been killed by this fungal disease.

In Antrim County, DED is estimated to have killed over 20% of the trees within our hardwood forests. Only a few remaining trees exist today.

Beech Bark Disease (BBD)

We are all familiar with what the Emerald Ash Borer did to our forests; next on the list of catastrophic pests is beech bark disease (BBD). Not really a disease, BBD is identified by a white powder on the limbs and main stem of a tree. BBD is a scale insect from Europe that has made its way across the country to Antrim County.

Although beech trees are not as significant economically as ash trees, they are extremely significant to the forest ecology, specifically to wildlife. The management of the beech trees in county forests revolved around retaining them for wildlife purposes.

Beech trees on county forest lands were removed preemptively on much of the Glacial Hills's property in 2016. The removal of beech on this parcel revolved around the heavy recreational use of this property, resulting in the trees being removed for safety reasons.

On all remaining forest lands, infected beech is being removed in combination with other cutting practices occurring on the properties. No salvage cutting of beech has been implemented to date.

Emerald Ash Borer (EAB)

The insect known as the emerald ash borer was discovered in southeast Michigan in 2002. Again, this invasive pest was thought to have been introduced to this country through packaging or shipping materials from Asia. By 2018, this insect had decimated ash tree populations throughout the United States.

In Antrim County, the EAB killed 99% of the ash trees within the county. It is unknown how this insect will impact forests in the future.

Example

On many of the county forest lands, ash trees represented roughly 25% of the trees and were considered an important asset to the forest both ecologically and economically.

Between the years 2006 and 2016, the forester conducted several salvage cutting operations to recover as much value as possible from the declining trees. Roughly 198,000 board feet of ash were recovered from county lands within this period.

This volume represented thousands of trees being removed from the forests. The Alba Road, Leonard Road, Glacial Hills Pathway and Natural Area, and Dickerson Road properties made up the bulk of the ash resources removed.

Forest Tent Caterpillars

2010 marked a catastrophic outbreak of the forest tent caterpillar throughout much of Northern Michigan. The outbreak began developing around 2006 when many began noticing a few caterpillars crawling around. Seemingly harmless, they went relatively unnoticed. In most instances, they were misidentified as the eastern tent caterpillar.

Numbers exponentially increased each year. In May and June of 2009, the distinct sound of caterpillar feces falling from the canopy was being reported throughout most of the region. Larger blocks of forest lands were becoming visibly defoliated. In 2010, caterpillar numbers exploded, and the previously defoliated areas merged, causing defoliation over most of the hardwood forest here in Northern Lower Michigan.

Most forest professionals recognized the insect as a native pest that should run a one- or two-year cycle and then fade away, not causing too much damage for another fifteen years or so. Starvation, parasitic flies, and bacteria would eventually collapse the population.

Having been through this before, there seemed to be no real concerns about tree health or our forests; "the trees will recover" was a common reply from many scientists and foresters. Unfortunately, we were wrong about that in many instances.

Mike Meriwether recounts this event as follows:

> I first encountered the forest tent caterpillars in the late 1980s. My memory does not serve me well, but I believe it was 1989 when the entire Jordan Valley was defoliated. This outbreak did not include the western portions of Antrim County. Defoliation seemed to have been contained east on M-66. It seemed short and uneventful at the time, an interesting point of conversation for the coffee shop. Many locals do not even remember the outbreak.
>
> Twenty years later, and after the second event in my lifetime, it turns out that these native bugs can have a devastating effect on our northern hardwood forest. I spent the months of June, July, and August 2010, inspecting woodlots that had been impacted by the forest tent caterpillar. Some similarities began to pop up. In some areas, late spring frost, high spring heat, drought, and caterpillars may have combined forces, killing thousands of trees. Other woodlots had as much as 10% mortality, with more trees stressed to the point where they may not recover. There is also some speculation that woodlots thinned within the past five years were the most vulnerable.

Forest pests continue to emerge and impact many of our forests. Oak wilt, hemlock woolly adelgid, and the longhorn beetle are new concerns within our forest. For more information on invasive species, please see: Michigan.gov/InvasiveSpecies.

Private Lands Assistance

It is significant that forestry technical assistance began to take hold in the 1980s. Although much of the forest land had been converted to agricultural uses, private forest land acreages still represented over 40% of the land ownership in Antrim County.

Prime Forest Land Project

In 1982, a collaborative effort to identify the economic and other benefits of our regional forest lands was undertaken. This project was called the Northwest Michigan Prime Forest Lands Identification Project. This project was quite innovative for its time. It included a regional steering committee, implementation committee, technical committee, and an information and education committee. These committees were made up of representatives from all Northern Lower Michigan communities and interest groups.

The project identifies the importance of the forest resources in Northern Lower Michigan. **Over 10 million acres (55%) of the region was identified as private non-industrial forest lands.**

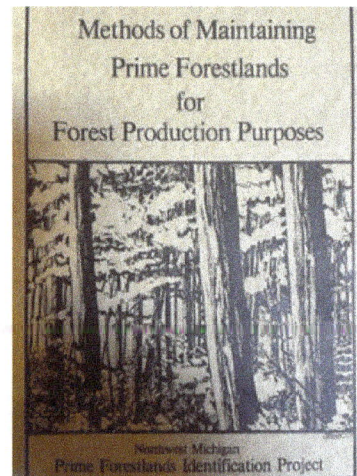

Methods of Maintaining Prime Forestlands for Forest Production Purposes

Northwest Michigan Prime Forestlands Identification Project

Providing technical assistance to private forest landowners was an important recommendation within the report. It was said, "Proper management of forest lands will improve the quality of timber products and often double or triple the quantity of timber that is growing. Most forest management practices that improve the forest land for timber products also improve soil, water handling properties of the forest and conditions for wildlife."

Technical assistance was available to private landowners from several sources at the time. The MDNR was the lead agency through its Cooperative Forest Management (CFM) program. Tom Stone was assigned to Antrim County through the CFM program. Tom was an outstanding resource to the Antrim Conservation District at the time. Any discussions regarding private land assistance in the region should have included Tom Stone. Other agencies included Soil Conservation Service (SCS), Soil Conservation Districts (SCD), industrial foresters, and consulting foresters. Michigan State University's Cooperative Extension Service provided educational opportunities for private landowners.

Tom Stone (far left)

Financial assistance, or cost sharing, for forest landowners was being provided by the Agricultural Stabilization and Conservation Service (ASCS). Forestry incentives were authorized by congress for the planting of trees, timber stand improvements, windbreaks, and other stewardship practices on private forest lands.

The funding of technical assistance foresters was a huge step forward in addressing how forest were being utilized. Equally important was the allocation of practice dollars which stimulated the planting of millions of trees and the thinning of thousands of acres of privately owned forests.

MANAGING OUR FORESTS IN THE FUTURE — TODAY'S FOREST MANAGEMENT

Property inventories, planning, harvesting, and management of forest resources on county-owned forest lands remains a priority today. Although some non-commercial improvement cutting is still occurring, most of the timber harvesting projects are commercial sales of forest products.

Inventories

Forest inventories are an important management tool for long-term planning purposes. Although several types of inventories were taken over the years, today the forester has utilized 1/20th acre sampling plots to determine the species, sizes, and densities within the county forests. These inventories are conducted before a planned harvest as well as post-harvest. The forest inventories are an attempt to define the current conditions, diameter distributions, species composition, trees per acre, and establish a cutting recommendation for each parcel. Once this information is gathered, tree marking for tree removal is focused on overstocked diameters within the forest. The goal is to move diameter distributions over time to an "uneven-aged" forest structure capable of sustainable growth.

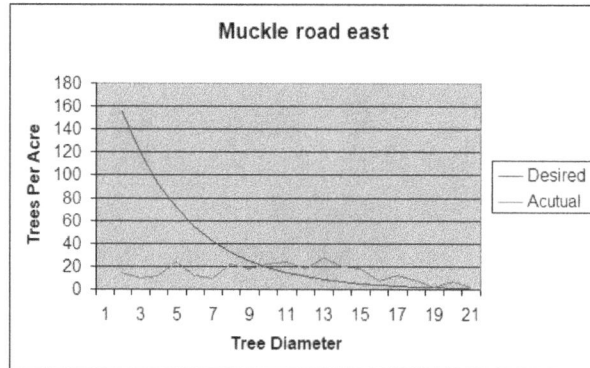

Muckle road east

Other silvicultural techniques are also employed where management of specific tree species, wildlife, or other methods are required. Aspen and pine management are examples.

Forest Management Plans

The ACD forester is responsible for developing and maintaining forest management plans for the county properties. These plans include a parcel history, types of forests, tree sizes, densities, cutting recommendations, information and recommendations for wildlife habitat improvements, fisheries, and recreational opportunities. Planning is only a template or guideline for potential outcomes and activities occurring on a parcel. These plans need to be adaptable to the changing forest dynamics occurring. They also need to be able to adapt to changing property usages, market trends, and most recently damaging agents such as insect and disease issues that have impacted forest planning.

Timber Sales

A cutting timeline for harvesting has been developed within the planning process (see Table 3). It is understood that the timeline for when and where to cut often considers market trends and damaging agents such as insects, diseases, and weather events.

Periodic timber sales are expected to continue. The sale of forest products is done to improve all aspects of the forest ecology. As our forests continue to grow and develop, they are expected to produce higher valued forest products on a sustainable basis. Protecting growing stock and developing size class distributions capable of producing higher valued trees on a sustainable basis is an overriding goal for most of our county forest lands. Careful and wise management will be required to accomplish these goals.

In order to ensure that Antrim County forests are sustainable in the future, the following recommendations need to be implemented.

RECOMMENDATIONS

Forestry Program Goals

The Antrim County Forestry Program has established a strong foundation for sustainable forests. All management decisions need to take positive steps toward maintaining and enhancing this sustainability.

Ecological Goals
- Protecting unique features
- Restoring forest ecology
- Improving biological diversity
- Ensuring sustainable forests in Antrim County

Recreational Goals
- To protect open space
- To provide recreational opportunities

Forest Management Goals
- To demonstrate sustainable forest management activities
- To generate revenue through forest management activities

Forestry Program Recommendations

In order to ensure that Antrim County forests are sustainable in the future, the following recommendations need to be implemented in 2024.

#1 Forestry Committee
The Antrim County Board of Commissioners should consider the re-establishment of a committee to assist with the planning and management of county forest lands, park, and natural areas.

#2 Forest Fund Policies
The forestry committee needs to develop policies for the forestry fund. As this fund continues to grow, these dollars must be protected and specific criteria for making decisions about the forests should be put in place by the Antrim County Board of Commissioners.

#3 Consolidation—New Acquisitions
The Forestry Committee should consolidate more forest lands into management areas. Here are a few priority areas:
- Mohrmann Park / Muckle Road / Dickerson Road (completed 2024)
- Lewis Road
- Barnes Park
- Lore Road

#4 Property Management
Antrim County should continue the formal relationship with the Antrim Conservation District and support the county forester.

#5 Management Plans
The county forester needs to upgrade parcel recommendations within each forest management plan.

#6 Parks and Recreation

To ensure consistent, long-term management of forest areas, natural areas, and park lands, the Antrim County Board of Commissioners needs to incorporate parks and recreation into the Antrim County Forestry Program.

#7 New Acquisitions

Antrim County Board of Commissioners needs to acquire properties on the east side of the county.

SUMMARY

Today the parks, natural areas, and forest land acreage contribute to Antrim County's natural beauty by protecting water quality and open spaces, plus offering a wealth of recreational opportunities for the community.

Maybe most impressive is the rich legacy of people who have dedicated both time and money to the acquisition and wise use of these properties.

The Antrim County forest land acquired under the Municipal Forest Reserve Act are often overlooked when compared to more publicized parcels such as the Grass River Natural Area, Antrim Creek, the Cedar River Natural Area, and Barnes Park.

County forests differ from parks and natural areas because they are able to generate their own revenue and do not rely on donations or usage fees. Usage is also relatively unregulated currently. To date, hunting, hiking, mushroom hunting, bird watching, and other passive recreational use are allowed in the county forests. Also allowed on many parcels is drive-in access by car, truck, or ORV.

In addition to providing natural resource opportunities, the county forests have been impactful by providing revenue that have supported the acquisition and maintenance of many of the parks, lands, and natural areas owned by the county.

Antrim County forest lands are expected to continue to produce revenue for the county. How these revenue are utilized will have significant impacts on the forest lands and the county.

As the county continues to grow and develop, it must guard against the temptation to sell, trade, or convert these properties to other uses. At first glance, many may wonder why the county owns and has invested millions of dollars in these properties. Hopefully, this publication can shine some light on this question and convince skeptics about the value of public property ownership.

In addition, these properties have been able to pay for themselves through careful forest management activities that have generated hundreds of thousands of dollars. Forest revenues have been used to purchase, maintain, and improve our parks and lands and have supplemented many community projects.

Today, we own some of the most productive and beautiful forests, parks, and natural areas in the state. Through its many land acquisitions, the county has protected forests, wetlands, and wildlife habitats. In addition, these lands provide recreational opportunities for the public and visitors to the county.

As this community continues to grow—I wonder how valuable these lands will be to the public in another eighty-seven years? I wonder if our current generations will have the same vision and stewardship ethics as our past generations.

I continue to be a proponent of forest stewardship, protecting public land acquisitions, and encouraging future acquisitions—not because I value them today—but because I know what value to our community they will have in the future.

Mike Meriwether
Forester
1986–Present

ACKNOWLEDGMENTS

Thanks are owed to the Antrim County Board of Commissioners, who have been dedicated to the vision of public lands for public enjoyment for generations to come.

Special thanks to Margaret "PEG" Comfort for helping with editing, structure, and formatting.

Special thanks to Julie at the equalization office for preparing maps for this document.

The following individuals have been involved with our county forests:

Everett Ash	Raymond Murphy
Albert Barnes	George Ourvey
Hans DeYoung	Curtis Patrick
Lee Ekstrom	Janet Pearson
Conrad Friedman	Bob and Brenda Ricksgers
Peter Garwood	Henry Ricksgers
HS Gibbs	Versal Shooks
Abdeen Jabara	Sharon Shumaker
Walter Kirkpatrick	Laura Stanek
Charlie Koop	Burt Stanley
Avid Johnson	Tom Stone
Carl Larson	Warren Studley
Jack Lockwood	Willard Vanderark
Ron Meeder	Jack White
Scott Morrison	Pete Wilks

ANTRIM CONSERVATION DISTRICT BOARD OF DIRECTORS 2023–2024

Bryan Smith, Chairman
Zach Gosnell, Vice Chairman
Adrienne Wolff, Treasurer
Randy Johnson, Director
Kathleen Peterson, Director

www.ingramcontent.com/pod-product-compliance
Lightning Source LLC
Chambersburg PA
CBHW080421030426
42335CB00020B/2532